Victim Services

Serving Victims of Crime and Other Traumatizing Events

To assist with 40 hour training requirements

Lorrie A Wnuk

Produced by Crisis Education Systems LLC

2014

Book design by Lorrie A Wnuk

Serving Victims of Crime and Other Traumatizing Events

Victims come in all forms. I have never met a victim that was in any way the same as any other victim I have worked with. I have responded to multiple domestic violence calls, fatal accidents and suicides...none of them were the same and yet all had similarities. This book is designed to help you deal with these types of incidents in a way that comes easier. It will help you understand the dynamics of victimization, critical incident stress and assessing the level of danger a victim may be in.

I have tried to incorporate the essentials to dealing with victims and survivors so that if you are working within law enforcement, a safe house or even a crisis hotline, you will be given information that you will find helpful and understandable.

There are great teachers out there that have taught me many things about serving victims and what to expect. I can only hope to pass on the information I have learned and used in a way that also benefits you and those you serve.

"Helping others is not a way to cure you; it is a way to help others cure themselves"

Lorrie A Wnuk
Crisis Education Systems LLC

Contents

Chapter One…………………………………………3   History Lesson

Chapter Two……………………………………15   Crime Victims Rights

Chapter Three…………………………………18   Critical Incident Stress

Chapter Four……………………………………24   Domestic Violence

Chapter Five……………………………………33   Stalking

Chapter six………………………………….…37   Sexual Assaults

Chapter Seven…………………………….……40   Threat Assessments

Chapter Eight…………………………….....…42   Special Populations

Chapter Nine...…………………………………56   Victimology

Chapter Ten.………………………………….…63   Educating Our Victims

Chapter Eleven……………………………….…73   Suicide

Chapter Twelve…………………………….……78   Criminal Justice System

Chapter Thirteen…………………………….…..87   Victim Compensation

Chapter Fourteen………………………………..90   Death Notifications

Chapter Fifteen………………………………….95   Self Care

Chapter Sixteen…………………………………98   Elder Abuse

Chapter One

A Little History Lesson on Victim Services

"Never doubt that a small group of thoughtful, committed citizens can change the world. Indeed, it's the only thing that ever has." Margaret Mead

Compiled by the National Center for Victims of Crime with the support and assistance of the U.S. Department of Justice Office for Victims of Crime, Victims' Assistance Legal Organization, Inc. (VALOR), and the many national, state and local victim service providers who offered documentation of their key victims' rights landmark activities.

In 1965 The first crime victim compensation program is established in California. By 1970, five additional compensation programs are created -- New York, Hawaii, Massachusetts, Maryland and the Virgin Islands.

In 1972 The first three victim assistance programs are created: Aid for Victims of Crime in St. Louis, Missouri; Bay Area Women Against Rape in San Francisco, California; and Rape Crisis Center in Washington, D.C.

In 1974 The Federal Law Enforcement Assistance Administration (LEAA) funds the first victim/witness programs in the Brooklyn and Milwaukee District Attorneys' offices, plus seven others through a grant to the National District Attorneys Association, to create model programs of assistance for victims, encourage victim cooperation, and improve prosecution.
The first law enforcement-based victim assistance programs are established in Fort Lauderdale, Florida and Indianapolis, Indiana. The U.S. Congress passes the *Child Abuse Prevention and Treatment Act* which establishes the National Center on Child Abuse and Neglect (NCCAN). The new Center creates an information clearinghouse, provides technical assistance and model programs.

In 1975 The first "Victims' Rights Week" is organized by the Philadelphia District Attorney. Citizen activists from across the country unite to expand victim services and increase recognition of victims' rights through the formation of the National Organization for Victim Assistance (NOVA).

In 1976 The National Organization for Women forms a task force to examine the problem of battering. It demands research into the problem, along with money for battered women's shelters. Nebraska becomes the first state to abolish the marital rape exemption.

The first national conference on battered women is sponsored by the Milwaukee Task Force on Women in Milwaukee, Wisconsin. In Fresno County, California, Chief Probation Officer James Rowland creates the first victim impact statement to provide the judiciary with an objective inventory of victim injuries and losses prior to sentencing. Women's Advocates in St. Paul, Minnesota starts the first hotline for battered women. Women's Advocates and Haven House in Pasadena, California establish the first shelters for battered women.

In 1977 The National Association of Crime Victim Compensation Boards is established by the existing 22 compensation programs to promote the creation of a nationwide network of compensation programs. Oregon becomes the first state to enact mandatory arrest in domestic violence cases.

In 1978 The National Coalition Against Sexual Assault (NCASA) is formed to combat sexual violence and promote services for rape victims. The National Coalition Against Domestic Violence (NCADV) is organized as a voice for the battered women's movement on a national level. NCADV initiates the introduction of the *Family Violence Prevention and Services Act* in the U.S. Congress. Parents of Murdered Children (POMC), a self-help support group, is founded in Cincinnati, Ohio. Minnesota becomes the first state to allow probable cause (warrantless) arrest in cases of domestic assault, regardless of whether a protection order had been issued.

In 1979 Frank G. Carrington, considered by many to be "the father of the victims' rights movement," founds the Crime Victims' Legal Advocacy Institute, Inc., to promote the rights of crime victims in the civil and criminal justice systems. The nonprofit organization was renamed VALOR, the Victims' Assistance Legal Organization, Inc., in 1981. The Office on Domestic Violence is established in the U.S. Department of Health and Human Services, but is later closed in 1981. The U.S. Congress fails to enact the Federal Law Enforcement Assistance Administration (LEAA) and federal funding for victims' programs is phased out. Many grassroots and "system-based" programs close.

In 1980 Mothers Against Drunk Driving (MADD) is founded after the death of 13-year-old Cari Lightner, who was killed by a repeat offender drunk driver. The first two MADD chapters are created in Sacramento, California and Annapolis, Maryland.
The U.S. Congress passes the *Parental Kidnapping Prevention Act of 1980.* Wisconsin passes the first *"Crime Victims' Bill of Rights."* The First National Day of Unity in October is established by NCADV to mourn battered women who have died, celebrate women who have survived the violence, and honor all who have worked to defeat domestic violence. This Day becomes Domestic Violence Awareness Week and, in 1987, expands to a month of awareness activities each October.

NCADV holds its first national conference in Washington, D.C., which gains federal recognition of critical issues facing battered women, and sees the birth of several state coalitions. The first Victim Impact Panel is sponsored by Remove Intoxicated Drivers (RID) in Oswego County, New York.

In 1981 Ronald Reagan becomes the first President to proclaim "Crime Victims' Rights Week" in April. The disappearance and murder of missing child Adam Walsh prompts a national campaign to raise public awareness about child abduction and enact laws to better protect children. The Attorney General's Task Force on Violent Crime recommends that a separate Task Force be created to consider victims' issues.

In 1982 In a Rose Garden ceremony, President Reagan appoints the Task Force on Victims of Crime, which holds public hearings in six cities across the nation to create a greatly needed

national focus on the needs of crime victims. The Task Force *Final Report* offers 68 recommendations that become the framework for the advancement of new programs and policies. Its final recommendation, to amend the Sixth Amendment of the U.S. Constitution to guarantee that "...the victim, in every criminal prosecution, shall have the right to be present and to be heard at all critical stages of judicial proceedings...," becomes a vital source of new energy pushing toward the successful efforts to secure state constitutional amendments through the 1980s and beyond. The *Federal Victim and Witness Protection Act of 1982* brings "fair treatment standards" to victims and witnesses in the federal criminal justice system.
California voters overwhelmingly pass Proposition 8, which guarantees restitution and other statutory reforms to crime victims.

The passage of the *Missing Children's Act of 1982* helps parents guarantee that identifying information on their missing child is promptly entered into the FBI National Crime Information Center (NCIC) computer system. The first Victim Impact Panel sponsored by MADD, which educates drunk drivers about the devastating impact of their criminal acts, is organized in Rutland, Massachusetts.

In 1983 The Office for Victims of Crime (OVC) is created by the U.S. Department of Justice within the Office of Justice Programs to implement recommendations from the President's Task Force on Victims of Crime. OVC establishes a national resource center, trains professionals, and develops model legislation to protect victims' rights. The U.S. Attorney General establishes a Task Force on Family Violence, which holds six public hearings across the United States. The U.S. Attorney General issues guidelines for federal victim and witness assistance. In April, President Reagan honors crime victims in a White House Rose Garden ceremony.

The First National Conference of the Judiciary on Victims of Crime is held at the National Judicial College in Reno, Nevada, with support from the National Institute of Justice. Conferees develop recommendations for the judiciary on victims' rights and services. President Reagan proclaims the first National Missing Children's Day in observance of the disappearance of missing child Etan Patz. The International Association of Chiefs of Police Board of Governors adopts a Crime Victims' Bill of Rights and establishes a victims' rights committee to bring about renewed emphasis on the needs of crime victims by law enforcement officials nationwide.

In 1984 The passage of the *Victims Of Crime Act* (VOCA) establishes the Crime Victims Fund, made up of federal criminal fines, penalties and bond forfeitures, to support state victim compensation and local victim service programs. President Reagan signs the *Justice Assistance Act*, which establishes a financial assistance program for state and local government and funds 200 new victim service programs. The *National Minimum Drinking Age Act of 1984* is enacted, providing strong incentives to states without "21" laws to raise the minimum age for drinking, saving thousands of young lives in years to come The first of several international affiliates of MADD is chartered in Canada. The National Center for Missing and Exploited Children (NCMEC) is created as the national resource for missing children. Passage of the *Missing Children's Assistance Act* pro-vides a Congressional mandate for the Center.
The Spiritual Dimension in Victim Services is founded to involve the religious community in violence prevention and victim assistance. Crime Prevention Week in February is marked by a White House ceremony with McGruff. The Task Force on Family Violence presents its report to

the U.S. Attorney General with recommendations for action, including: the criminal justice system's response to battered women; prevention and awareness; education and training; and data collection and reporting. The U.S. Congress passes the *Family Violence Prevention and Services Act*, which earmarks federal funding for programs serving victims of domestic violence. The ad-hoc committee on the constitutional amendment formalizes its plans to secure passage of amendments at the state level.

Concerns of Police Survivors (COPS) is organized at the first police survivors' seminar held in Washington, D.C. by 110 relatives of officers killed in the line of duty. The first National Symposium on Sexual Assault is co-sponsored by the Office of Justice Programs and the Federal Bureau of Investigation, highlighting on the federal level the important needs of victims of rape and sexual assault.

A victim/witness notification system is established within the Federal Bureau of Prisons. The Office for Victims of Crime hosts the first national symposium on child molestation. Victim/witness Coordinator positions are established in the U.S. Attorneys' offices within the U.S. Department of Justice. California State University-Fresno initiates the first Victim Services Certificate Program offered for academic credit by a university. Remove Intoxicated Drivers (RID) calls for a comprehensive Sane National Alcohol Policy (SNAP) to curb aggressive promotions aimed at youth.

OVC establishes the National Victims Resource Center, now named the Office for Victims of Crime Resource Center (OVCRC) to serve as a clearinghouse for OVC publications and other resource information.

In 1985 The Federal Crime Victims Fund deposits total $68 million. The National Victim Center is founded in honor of Sunny von Bulow to promote the rights and needs of crime victims, and to educate Americans about the devastating effect of crime on our society. The United Nations General Assembly passes the *International Declaration on the Rights of Victims of Crime and the Abuse of Power*. President Reagan announces a Child Safety Partnership with 26 members. Its mission is to enhance private sector efforts to promote child safety, to clarify information about child victimization, and to increase public awareness of child abuse. The U.S. Surgeon General issues a report identifying domestic violence as a major public health problem.

In 1986 The Office for Victims of Crime awards the first grants to support state victim compensation and assistance programs.

Two years after its passage, the *Victims of Crime Act* is amended by the *Children's Justice Act* to provide funds specifically for the investigation and prosecution of child abuse. Over 100 constitutional amendment supporters meet in Washington, D.C. at a forum sponsored by NOVA to refine a national plan to secure state constitutional amendments for victims of crime.

Rhode Island passes a constitutional amendment granting victims the right to restitution, to submit victim impact statements, and to be treated with dignity and respect. Compensation programs have been established in thirty-five states. MADD's "Red Ribbon Campaign" enlists motorists to display a red ribbon on their automobiles, pledging to drive safe and sober during the holidays. This national public awareness effort has since become an annual campaign.

In 1987 The Victims' Constitutional Amendment Network (VCAN) and Steering Committee is formed at a meeting hosted by the National Victim Center. Security on Campus, Inc. (SOC) is established by Howard and Connie Clery, following the tragic robbery, rape and murder of their daughter Jeanne at Lehigh University in Pennsylvania. SOC raises national awareness about the hidden epidemic of violence on our nation's campuses. The American Correctional Association establishes a Task Force on Victims of Crime. NCADV establishes the first national toll-free domestic violence hotline. Victim advocates in Florida, frustrated by five years of inaction on a proposed constitutional amendment by their legislature, begin a petition drive. Thousands of citizens sign petitions supporting constitutional protection for victims' rights. The Florida legislature reconsiders, and the constitutional amendment appears on the 1988 ballot.

In 1988 OVC establishes funds for the Victim Assistance in Indian Country (VAIC) grant program to provide direct services to Native Americans by establishing "on-reservation" victim assistance programs in Indian Country. The National Aging Resource Center on Elder Abuse (NARCEA) is established in a cooperative agreement among the American Public Welfare Association, the National Association of State Units on Aging, and the University of Delaware. Renamed the National Center on Elder Abuse, it continues to provide information and statistics.

State v. Ciskie is the first case to allow the use of expert testimony to explain the behavior and mental state of an adult rape victim. The testimony is used to show why a victim of repeated physical and sexual assaults by her intimate partner would not immediately call the police or take action. The jury convicts the defendant on four counts of rape. The *Federal Drunk Driving Prevention Act* is passed, and states raise the minimum drinking age to 21. Constitutional amendments are introduced in Arizona, California, Connecticut, Delaware, Michigan, South Carolina and Washington. Florida's amendment is placed on the November ballot where it passes with 90% of the vote. Michigan's constitutional amendment passes with over 80% of the vote. The first "Indian Nations: Justice for Victims of Crime" conference is sponsored by the Office for Victims of Crime in Rapid City, South Dakota. VOCA amendments legislatively establish the Office for Victims of Crime, elevate the position of Director by making Senate confirmation necessary for appointment, and induce state compensation programs to cover victims of domestic violence, homicide and drunk driving. In addition, VOCA amendments added a new "priority" category of funding victim assistance programs at the behest of MADD and POMC for "previously underserved victims of crime." OVC also establishes a Federal Emergency Fund for victims in the federal criminal justice system.

In 1989 The legislatures in Texas and Washington pass their respective constitutional amendments, which are both ratified by voters in November. OVC provides funding for the first time to the National Association of Crime Victim Compensation Boards to expand national training and technical assistance efforts.

In 1990 The Federal Crime Victims Fund deposits total over $146 million. The U.S. Congress passes the *Hate Crime Statistics Act* requiring the U.S. Attorney General to collect data of incidence of certain crimes motivated by prejudice based on race, religion, sexual orientation or ethnicity. The *Student Right-to-Know and Campus Security Act*, requiring institutions of higher education to disclose murder, rape, robbery and other crimes on campus, is signed into law by President Bush. The *Victims of Child Abuse Act of 1990*, which features reforms to make the federal criminal justice system less traumatic for child victims and witnesses, is passed by the U.S. Congress. The *Victims' Rights and Restitution Act of 1990* incorporates a Bill of Rights for federal crime victims and codifies services that should be available to victims of crime. U.S. Congress passes legislation proposed by MADD to prevent drunk drivers and other offenders from filing bankruptcy to avoid paying criminal restitution or civil fines.

The Arizona petition drive to place the victims' rights constitutional amendment on the ballot succeeds, and it is ratified by voters. The first *National Incidence Study on Missing, Abducted, Runaway and Throwaway Children in America* shows that over one million children fall victim to abduction annually. The *National Child Search Assistance Act* requires law enforcement to enter reports of missing children and unidentified persons in the NCIC computer.

In 1991 U.S. Representative Ilena Ros-Lehtinen (R-FL) files the first Congressional Joint Resolution to place victims' rights in the U.S. Constitution. The *Violence Against Women Act of 1991* is considered by the U.S. Congress. California State University-Fresno approves the first Bachelors Degree Program in Victimology in the nation. The *Campus Sexual Assault Victims' Bill of Rights Act* is introduced in the U.S. Congress. The results of the first national public opinion poll to examine citizens' attitudes about violence and victimization, *America Speaks Out*, are released by the National Victim Center during National Crime Victims' Rights Week. The Attorney General's Summit on Law Enforcement and Violent Crime focuses national attention on victims' rights in the criminal justice system. The U.S. Attorney General issues new comprehensive guidelines that establish procedures for the federal criminal justice system to respond to the needs of crime victims. The 1991 Attorney General Guidelines for Victim and Witness Assistance implement new protections of the *Crime Control Act of 1990*, integrating the requirements of the *Federal Crime Victims' Bill of Rights*, the *Victims of Child Abuse Act* and the *Victim and Witness Protection Act of 1982*. The first national conference that addresses crime victims' rights and needs in corrections is sponsored by the Office for Victims of Crime in California.

The first International Conference on Campus Sexual Assault is held in Orlando, Florida. The American Probation and Parole Association (APPA) establishes a Victim Issues Committee to examine victims' issues and concerns related to community corrections.
The *International Parental Child Kidnapping Act* makes the act of unlawfully removing a child outside the United States a federal felony. The Spiritual Dimension in Victim Services facilitates a conference of leaders of 13 religious denominations to plan ways in which these large religious bodies can increase awareness of crime victims' needs and provide appropriate services.
The New Jersey legislature passes a victims' rights constitutional amendment, which is ratified by voters in November.
Colorado legislators introduce a constitutional amendment on the first day of National Crime Victims' Rights Week. Fifteen days later, the bill is unanimously passed by both Houses to be placed on the ballot in 1992.
In an 8-0 decision, the U.S. Supreme Court ruled in *Simon & Schuster v. New York Crime Victims Board* that New York's notoriety-for-profit statute was overly broad and, in the final analysis, unconstitutional. Notoriety-for-profit statutes had been passed by many states at this time to prevent convicted criminals from profiting from the proceeds of depictions of their crime in the media or publications. States must now review their existing statutes to come into compliance with the Supreme Court's decision.

By the end of 1991, seven states have incorporated victims' rights into their state constitutions. OVC provides funding to the National Victim Center for *Civil Legal Remedies for Crime Victims* to train victim advocates nationwide on additional avenues for victims to seek justice within the civil justice system.

In 1992 *Rape in America: A Report to the Nation*, published during National Crime Victims' Rights Week by the National Crime Victims Research and Treatment Center and the National Victim Center, clarifies the scope and devastating effect of rape in this nation, including the fact that 683,000 women are raped annually in the United States. The Association of Paroling Authorities, International establishes a Victim Issues Committee to examine victims' needs, rights and services in parole processes.

The U.S. Congress reauthorizes the *Higher Education Bill* which includes the *Campus Sexual Assault Victims' Bill of Rights.*

The *Battered Women's Testimony Act,* which urges states to accept expert testimony in criminal cases involving battered women, is passed by Congress and signed into law by President Bush.

In a unanimous decision, the U.S. Supreme Court -- in *R.A.V. vs. City of St. Paul* -- struck down a local hate crimes ordinance in Minnesota.

Five states -- Colorado, Kansas, Illinois, Missouri and New Mexico -- ratify constitutional amendments for victims' rights.

Twenty-eight states pass anti-stalking legislation. Massachusetts passes a landmark bill creating a statewide computerized domestic violence registry and requires judges to check the registry when handling such cases.

The first national conference is convened, using OVC funds, that brings together representatives from VOCA victim assistance and victim compensation programs.

In 1993 Wisconsin ratifies its constitutional amendment for victims' rights, bringing the total number of states with these amendments to 14. President Clinton signs the "Brady Bill" requiring a waiting period for the purchase of handguns. Congress passes the *Child Sexual Abuse Registry Act* establishing a national repository for information on child sex offenders.

Twenty-two states pass stalking statutes, bringing the total number of states with stalking laws to 50, plus the District of Columbia.

In 1994 The American Correctional Association Victims Committee publishes the landmark *Report and Recommendations on Victims of Juvenile Crime*, which offers guidelines for improving victims' rights and services when the offender is a juvenile.

Six additional states pass constitutional amendments for victims' rights -- the largest number ever in a single year -- bringing the total number of states with amendments to 20. States with new amendments include: Alabama, Alaska, Idaho, Maryland, Ohio, and Utah.

President Clinton signs a comprehensive package of federal victims' rights legislation as part of the *Violent Crime Control and Law Enforcement Act.* The *Act* includes: *Violence Against Women Act*, which authorizes more than $1 billion in funding for programs to combat violence against women. Enhanced VOCA funding provisions were enacted. The establishment of a National Child Sex Offender Registry took place and enhanced sentences for drunk drivers with child passengers.

Kentucky becomes the first state to institute automated telephone voice notification to crime victims of their offender's status and release date. OVC establishes the Community Crisis

Response (CCR) program, using the NOVA model, to improve services to victims of violent crimes in communities that have experienced crimes resulting in multiple victimizations.

In 1995 The Federal Crime Victims Fund deposits total $233,907,256. Legislatures in three states -- Indiana, Nebraska, and North Carolina -- pass constitutional amendments which will be placed on the ballot in 1996. The National Victims' Constitutional Amendment Network proposes the first draft of language for a federal constitutional amendment for victims' rights. The U.S. Department of Justice convenes a national conference to encourage implementation of the *Violence Against Women Act.*
The first class graduates from the National Victim Assistance Academy in Washington, D.C. Supported by the Office for Victims of Crime, the university-based Academy provides an academically credited 45-hour curriculum on victimology, victims' rights and myriad other topics.

In 1996 Federal Victims' Rights Constitutional Amendments are introduced in both houses of Congress with bi-partisan support.
Both presidential candidates and the Attorney General endorse the concept of a Victims' Rights Constitutional Amendment.
The Federal Crime Victims Fund reaches an historic high with deposits over $525 million. Eight states ratify the passage of constitutional amendments for victims' rights -- raising the total number of state constitutional amendments to 29 nationwide.
The *Community Notification Act*, known as "Megan's Law," provides for notifying communities of the location of convicted sex offenders by amendment to the national *Child Sexual Abuse Registry* legislation.
President Clinton signs the *Antiterrorism and Effective Death Penalty Act* providing one million dollars in funding to strengthen antiterrorism efforts, making restitution mandatory in violent crime cases, and expanding the compensation and assistance services for victims of terrorism both at home and abroad, including victims in the military.
The Office for Victims of Crime uses its new authority under the *Antiterrorism and Effective Death Penalty Act to provide substantial financial assistance to the victims and survivors of the Oklahoma City bombing.*

The *Mandatory Victims' Restitution Act*, enacted as Title II of the *Antiterrorism and Effective Death Penalty Act*, allows federal courts to award "public harm" restitution directly to state VOCA victim assistance programs. As a result of the new sentencing guidelines, judges can require federal offenders in certain drug offense cases to pay "community restitution."
The National Domestic Violence Hotline is established to provide crisis intervention information and referrals to victims of domestic violence and their friends and family.
OVC launches a number of international crime victim initiatives including working to foster worldwide implementation of a United Nations declaration on victims' rights and working to better assist Americans who are victimized abroad.
The *Church Arson Prevention Act* is signed into law in July, in response to increasing numbers of acts of arson against religious institutions around the country. The *Drug-Induced Rape Prevention Act* is enacted to address the emerging issue of the use of sedating drugs by rapists on victims. The Office for Juvenile Justice and Delinquency Prevention (OJJDP) within the U.S. Department of Justice issues the *Juvenile Justice Action Plan* that includes recommendations for

victims' rights and services for victims of juvenile offenders within the juvenile justice system. President Clinton directs the Attorney General to hold the federal system to a higher standard of services for crime victims.

In 1997 In January, a federal victims' rights constitutional amendment is re-introduced in the opening days of the 105th Congress with strong bi-partisan support. In February, OVC convenes the first National Symposium on Victims of Federal Crimes. Coordinated by the National Organization for Victim Assistance, the symposium provides intensive training to nearly 1,000 federal employees who work with crime victims around the world. In March, Congress passes at historic speed the *Victims Rights Clarification Act of 1997* to clarify existing federal law allowing victims to attend a trial and to appear as "impact witnesses" during the sentencing phase of both capital and non-capital cases. Supported by the Justice Department, President Clinton immediately signs the *Act,* allowing the victims and survivors of the bombing of the Alfred P. Murrah Federal Building in Oklahoma City to both observe the trial that is scheduled to begin within days and to provide input later at sentencing. In April, the Senate Judiciary Committee conducts hearings on the proposed federal constitutional amendment. While not endorsing specific language, Attorney General Janet Reno testifies in support of federal constitutional rights for crime victims. In June, President Clinton reaffirms his support of federal constitutional rights for crime victims in a Rose Garden ceremony attended by members of Congress, criminal justice officials, and local, state, and national victims' rights organizations. Also that month, the Judiciary Committee in the U.S. House of Representatives conducts its first hearing on the proposed amendment.

In July, the *Crime Victims Assistance Act* is introduced into the U.S. Senate, offering full-scale reform of federal rules and federal law to establish stronger rights and protections for victims of federal crime. This legislation further proposes to assist victims of state crime through the infusion of additional resources to make the criminal justice system more supportive of crime victims.
To fully recognize the sovereignty of Indian Nations, OVC for the first time provides victim assistance grants in Indian Country directly to the tribes. A federal anti-stalking law is enacted by Congress. The Federal Crime Victims Fund reaches its second highest
year in fund collections with deposits totaling $363 million. Due to the large influx of VOCA funds in the previous fiscal year, OVC hosts a series of regional meetings with state VOCA administrators to encourage states to develop multi-year funding strategies to help stabilize local program funding, expand outreach to previously underserved victims, and to support the development and implementation of technologies to improve victims' rights and services. OVC continues its support of the victims and survivors of the bombing of the Alfred P. Murrah Federal Building in Oklahoma City by funding additional advocates, crisis counseling, and travel expenses to court proceedings for the bombing victims. When the venue of the trial is changed to Denver, Colorado, OVC provides funding for a special closed circuit broadcast to victims and survivors in Oklahoma City. OVC representatives join the United States Delegation to the United Nations Commission on Criminal Justice and Crime Prevention. OVC plays a leadership role in the development of an International Victim Assistance Training Manual to implement the *U.N. Declaration of Basic Principles of Justice for Victims of Crime and Abuse of Power.* The National Victim Center utilizes its extensive legislative database to create the *Legislative Sourcebook*, a comprehensive compendium of victims' rights laws in all states.

Developed with support from OVC, the *Sourcebook* becomes the definitive digest of state legislation on crime victims' rights laws for the nation. The third National Victim Assistance Academy is held, bringing the total number of students graduated to over 300 from 48 states. Supported by OVC and sponsored by the Victims' Assistance Legal Organization, California State University-Fresno, and the Medical University of South Carolina, the 45-hour Academy is conducted simultaneously at four universities across the nation linked by distance learning technology. A comprehensive national training for VOCA Compensation and Assistance programs is hosted by the National Association of Crime Victim Compensation Boards and the National Organization for Victim Assistance with support from OVC. VOCA representatives from *all* 50 states and every territory are in attendance. During National Crime Victims Rights Week, OVC officially launches its homepage <http://www.ojp.usdoj.gov/ovc/> providing Internet access to its comprehensive resources on victims' rights and services. *New Directions from the Field: Victims Rights and Services for the 21ˢᵗ Century* is completed with support from OVC. It assesses the nation's progress in meeting the recommendations set forth in the *Final Report* of the 1982 President's Task Force on Victims of Crime and issues over 250 new recommendations from the field for the next millennium.

In 1998 Senate Joint Resolution 44, a new version of the federal Victims' Rights Amendment, is introduced in the Senate by Senators Jon Kyl and Dianne Feinstein. The Senate Judiciary Committee subsequently approves SJR 44 by an 11-6 vote.
Four new states pass state victims' rights constitutional amendments: Louisiana by a voter margin of approval of 69%; Mississippi by 93%; Montana by 71%; and Tennessee by 89%. Also in 1998, the Supreme Court of Oregon overturns the Oregon state victims' rights amendment, originally passed in 1996, citing structural deficiencies. The fourth National Victim Assistance Academy (NVAA), sponsored and funded by the U.S. Department of Justice, Office for Victims of Crime, is held at four university sites around the country, bringing the total number of NVAA graduates to nearly 700. To date, students from all fifty states, one American territory, and three foreign countries have attended the Academy. PL 105-244, the Higher Education Amendments of 1998, is passed. Part E of this legislation, "Grants to Combat Violent Crimes Against Women on Campus," is authorized through the year 2003, and appropriates a total of $10 million in grant funding to the Violence Against Women Grants Office for fiscal year 1999. Another primary aim of this legislation is to reduce binge drinking and illegal alcohol consumption on college campuses.

In 1999 SJR 3, the Federal Victims' Rights Constitutional Amendment is introduced before the 106th Congress
The Victim Restitution Enforcement Act is introduced requiring mandatory restitution. Violence Against Women Act II is introduced before Congress. OVC issues first grants to create State Victim Assistance Academies. The National Crime Victim Bar association is formed by the National Center for Victims of Crime. The Federal Crime Victims Fund deposits total $985 million

In 2000 The Violence Against Women Act of 2000 is signed into law by President Clinton. The Internet Fraud Complaint Center website is created by the U.S. Department of Justice, FBI, & the National White Collar Crime Center. The Federal Victims' Rights Constitutional

Amendment (SJR 3) is addressed in the full Senate, but later withdrawn because of insufficient votes for approval. The U.S. Congress passes a new national drunk driving limit if 0.08. The Victims of Trafficking & Violence Protection Act (for immigrant victims) is passed. The Federal Crime Victims Fund deposits total $777 million

In 2001 Congress responds to the 9/11 terrorist acts with new laws providing tax relief, compensation, funding for new services & civil claims as part of the Air & Transportation Safety & System Stabilization Act & the USA Patriot Act of 2001. The reauthorization of the Violence Against Women Act of 1994 is passed with some expanded funding & services. The Child Abuse prevention & Enforcement Act & Jennifer's Law allows use of Byrne grant funds for prevention & costs of entering victims in FBI's NCIC database. The Federal Crime Victims Fund deposits total $544 million

In 2002 All 50 states, District of Columbia, US Virgin Islands, Puerto Rico, & Guam have established crime victim compensation programs. The National Association of VOCA Assistance Administrators is created and OVC sponsors. The National Public Awareness & Education Campaign to promote the scope & availability of victims' rights & services nationwide offers the first "Helping Outreach Programs to Expand" grants to grassroots, non-profit, community- based victim organizations to improve services & sponsors regional roundtables for victims. The Federal Crime Victims Fund deposits total $519 million

In 2003 The Office for Victims of Crime celebrates its 20th anniversary of service. The Senate Judiciary Committee passes the Federal Victims' Rights Constitutional Amendment: "But The House Fails to Take Action". Congress makes the Office on Violence Against Women a permanent independent office. The Protect Act of 2003 (Amber Alert) creates a national network of AMBER (America's Missing: Broadcast Emergency Response) to facilitate rapid law enforcement & community response to kidnapped or abducted children. Congress passes the Prison Rape Elimination Act to address the issue of rape in correctional institutions

In 2004 U.S. Congress passed the strongest federal crime victims' legislation in nation's history after failure to approve a Federal Constitutional Amendment; H.R. 5107, The Justice For All Act of 2004, strengthens the rights of victims of federal crimes and provides enforcement and remedies when there is failure to comply; Title 1 is named in honor of five victims: Scott Campbell, Stephanie Roper, Wendy Preston, Louarna Gillis and Nila Lynn; H.R. 5107 also includes provisions for DNA analysis backlog. The Senate Judiciary Committee passes the Federal Victims' Rights Constitutional Amendment: "But The House Fails to Take Action"

"When someone is a victim, he or she should be at the center of the criminal justice process, not on the outside looking in. Participation in all forms of government is the essence of democracy. Victims should be guaranteed the right to participate in proceedings related to crimes committed against them. People accused of crimes have explicit constitutional rights. Ordinary citizens have a constitutional right to participate in criminal trials by serving on a jury. The press has a constitutional right to attend trials. All of this is as it should be. It is only the victims of crime who have no constitutional right to participate, and that is not the way it should be."

President William Jefferson Clinton, Remarks at Announcement of Victims' Rights Constitutional Amendment June 25, 1996

Chapter Two

History of State Victims' Rights Constitutional Amendments

State	Year Passed	Electoral Support	State	Year Passed	Electoral Support
Alabama	1994	80%	Nebraska	1996	78%
Alaska	1994	87%	Nevada	1996	74%
Arizona	1990	58%	New Jersey	1991	85%
California	1982	56%	New Mexico	1992	68%
Colorado	1992	86%	North Carolina	1996	78%
Connecticut	1996	78%	Ohio	1994	77%
Florida	1988	90%	Oklahoma	1996	91%
Idaho	1994	79%	Oregon OVERTURNED	1996 1998	59%
Illinois	1992	77%			
Indiana	1996	89%	Rhode Island	1986	*
Kansas	1992	84%	South Carolina	1996	89%
Louisiana	1998	69%	Tennessee	1998	89%
Maryland	1994	92%	Texas	1989	73%
Michigan	1992	84%	Utah	1994	68%
Mississippi	1998	93%	Virginia	1996	84%
Missouri	1992	84%	Washington	1989	78%
Montana	1998	71%	Wisconsin	1993	84%

* Passed by Constitutional Convention.

This document was last updated on May 29, 2008
Provided by the Office for Victims of Crime

VICTIMS OF CRIME BILL OF RIGHTS FOR FEDERAL CASES.

A crime victim has the following rights.

The right to be treated with fairness and with respect for the victim's dignity and privacy;

The right to be reasonably protected from the accused offender;

The right to be notified of court proceedings;

The right to be present at all public court proceedings related to the offense, unless the court determines that testimony by the victim would be materially affected if the victim heard other testimony at trial;

The right to confer with the attorney for the Government in the case;

The right to restitution; and,

The right to information about the conviction, sentencing, imprisonment and release of the offender.

Special Rights

Some kinds of cases entitle victims to special notice and services.

Violent Crimes or Sexual Abuse

At sentencing victims of violent crimes or sexual abuse have the right of allocution, i.e. to make a statement or present information in relation to the offender's sentence, if they wish. The victim or victim's family may make a short statement to the court about the impact of the crime. The U.S. Attorney's Office will NOT pay for the victim or victim's family to attend the sentencing.

Federal Domestic Violence Offenses

In federal domestic violence cases, the victim must be given an opportunity to be heard prior to the defendant's release on bond. This requirement only applies in very limited cases where the defendant has been charged with a Federal Domestic Violence crime. It has no effect in state or local courts.

Sexual Assault

Victims of Sexual Assault who may be at risk of contracting the "AIDS" virus may request that the defendant be ordered to take the AIDS test. If this applies to you, contact the Assistant US Attorney who prosecuted your case or the Victim Advocate who worked with you. Again, this applies only to federally charged cases of sexual assault.

Important Notes

Involvement in the Victim Witness Program is VOLUNTARY. If you were the victim of a Federal Crime, you may be contacted by a Victim Advocate who will tell you that a defendant has been charged with the crime. You may be asked to fill out a "Pre-Trial Questionnaire" and a "Request For Notice". If you return the Request For Notice, you will be kept informed of major developments of the case as it goes through the Federal Courts.

Many Federal cases do not go to trial, the defendant may plead guilty before the trial. Whether a defendant pleads guilty or is convicted at trial, you will be notified of the results and the sentence that the defendant received. We will notify the Bureau of Prisons (BOP) of your interest in the case and the BOP will then notify you where the defendant will serve his/her jail term. The BOP will also tell you when the defendant is scheduled to be released, parole hearings, escapes, and other major events about the defendant.

In some cases, the Judge will order that restitution be paid to the victim(s) of the crime. If restitution was ordered to be paid by the defendant please be aware that it may take some time for you to get any money. Please read the separate section on this web page that addresses restitution issues.

A major problem that BOP and the courts face is keeping track of the victims. Many victims will move or changes addresses and not notify the court or BOP. This means that BOP can't notify victims of changes in the defendants' status or release dates. It also means that as restitution becomes available, it cannot be mailed to the victim. Please keep the court and BOP undated on any address changes.

Get to know what your state has on the books as far as victims rights are concerned....

Chapter Three

Working With Critical Incident Victims

What does it mean to work with someone that has just lived through a critical incident in their lives? First we need to define what a critical incident is. This is any event that puts distress onto the victim in a severe emotional level. It is anything that might be traumatizing for them and yet might not be for anyone else. We all have different things that may and do trigger an event of critical proportions.

They have experienced a traumatic event or a critical incident (any incident that causes people to experience unusually strong emotional reactions which have the potential to affect their ability to function at their workplace, within their families, and/or in other areas of their lives). This event or events may be time-limited or may be on-going or chronic. They can cause Post Traumatic Stress Disorders at that point.

Even though the event may be over, they may now be experiencing or may experience later, some strong emotional or physical reactions. It is very common, in fact quite normal, for people to experience emotional aftershocks when they have passed through a horrible event or be subject to ongoing stressors.

Sometimes the emotional after-shocks (or stress reactions) appear immediately after the traumatic event. Sometimes they may appear a few hours or a few days later. And, in some cases, weeks or months may pass before the stress reactions appear.

The signs and symptoms of a stress reaction may last a few days, a few weeks or a few months and occasionally longer, depending on the severity of the traumatic event. With understanding and the support of loved ones, the stress reactions usually pass more quickly. Occasionally, the traumatic event is so painful that professional assistance from a counselor may be necessary. This does not imply craziness or weakness. It simply indicates that the particular event was just too powerful for the person to manage by themselves. Here are some very common signs and signals of a stress reaction:

PHYSICAL: Fatigue, thirst, headaches, visual difficulties, vomiting, grinding of teeth, weakness, dizziness, profuse sweating, chills, rapid heart rate, nausea, muscle tremors, twitches, chest pain, * difficulty breathing, elevated blood pressures, * shock symptoms, fainting, etc. (*Indicates the need for medical evaluation).

COGNITIVE:(AFFECTING THOUGHTS): blaming someone, confusion, poor attention, poor decisions, heightened or lowered alertness, poor concentration, memory problems, hyper-vigilance, difficulty identifying familiar objects/people, increased or decreased awareness of surroundings, poor problem solving, poor abstract thinking, loss of time, place, or person orientation, disturbed thinking, nightmares, intrusive images, etc.

EMOTIONAL: anxiety, guilt, grief, denial, severe panic (rare), emotional shock, fear, uncertainty, loss of emotional control, depression, inappropriate emotional response, apprehension, feeling overwhelmed, intense anger, irritability, agitation, etc.

BEHAVIORAL: change in activity, change in speech patterns, withdrawal, emotional outbursts, suspiciousness, change in usual communications, loss or increase of appetite, alcohol consumption, inability to rest, antisocial acts, nonspecific bodily complaints, hyper-alertness to environment, intensification of startle reflex, pacing, erratic movements, change in sexual functioning, etc.

So now that we are aware of some of the most common signs and symptoms of a person suffering from Critical incident stress, we need to know how to deal with that person. The best thing to remember is that this person is not the same as you or I would be in a normal thinking environment with nothing stressing us out. When in a high stress state, we have a tendency to not think with our frontal lobe or what we refer to as our logical brain. The terms used to describe this type of thinking often reflect the Fight or Flight responses. If you keep this in mind at all times while working with a stressed out individual it will help you expect the unexpected and deal with the responses that can and do happen from time to time.

The best way to describe the "Fight" reaction is looking back at a death notification I had to give to a 17 year old girl after her mother had died. The moment I told her her mother was dead she hauled off and punched me. She punched me hard enough to knock me down. Then she fell to the floor and cried rocking herself, not even remembering the good right hook she had just given me. This was for sure a "Fight" response and it was immediate! Sometimes this response comes on a bit slower too. You may have a person acting completely rational and seems to be doing ok when all at once things take a turn for the worse. One of my employees was taking care of a woman whose child had died from several medical conditions. As she was calmly talking to her and providing support to her the woman suddenly got up off the steps she was sitting on and began to beat her head into the metal stair railing. This took place well into the call; it was not a sudden reaction.

The "Flight" reaction is also one that can come on fast or take some time to develop. Let's look at the case I had when the young lady had been sexually assaulted and she ran from everyone, including those that were trying to help her. As the "flight" reaction can come on quickly, like the "Fight" reaction, it may present itself later. We have been unable to locate victims a day or several weeks after an incident because they have moved into the "Flight" reaction and tried to get away from everything that was going on.

Another way of looking at the responses of stressed individuals is to consider they are unable to reason with or make sense out of what is happening or just happened. We will often keep hearing them utter words like, "why, why, why?" or "this isn't happening".

The stress reaction is definitely more than emotional, as there are neurochemical changes in the brain. People may be on guard, and over-reactive and unable to control their reactions. Younger people can be more vulnerable, and there are levels of stress reaction directly related to the amount of control each victim has over their situation.

Suppressed trauma may last for months or years, symptoms of which can include haunting memories, social withdrawal, and anxiety or depression. Feeling helpless and hopeless, victims may retreat into emotional detachment, experiencing psychological numbing. A lack of outward symptomology falsely reassures the casual observer that there has been no disruption in an individual's life, but this appearance of coping through emotional distancing represents a larger problem, since the stressors are still active.

This is an important area to learn as the jobs you do working with victims and others that are traumatized may cause great stress for you as well. What you are helping others deal with can and will become a stressor for you in ways you may have never expected. If you are called to assist someone that may have similar things in their life to yours, it is often times hard to not draw parallels to your own life and have difficulty separating them. Also if you witness a scene that is grizzly or not a "normal" scene, you may experience bad dreams and other symptoms of critical incident stress.

Critical Incident Stress Management (CISM) provides help for those affected. It focuses on the aftermath of critical incidents. CISM teams initiate and encourage the type of conversation that provides an emotional outlet. All discussions are strictly confidential. No notes are taken and no critique is made of the operations. The focus is on the emotional repercussions of the situation. This process of debriefing was designed by Dr. Jeffrey Mitchell in 1989, whose structured format of "talking it out" is recognized as the standard in the industry for CIS Management.

Below are some lists of common reactions to critical incident stress.

SIGNS AND SYMPTOMS OF CRITICAL INCIDENT STRESS

Physical*	Cognitive	Emotional	Behavioral
chills	confusion	fear	withdrawal
thirst	nightmares	guilt	antisocial acts
fatigue	uncertainty	grief	inability to rest
nausea	hyper vigilance	panic	intensified pacing
fainting	suspiciousness	denial	erratic movements
twitches	intrusive images	anxiety	change in social activity
vomiting	blaming someone	agitation	change in speech patterns
dizziness	poor problem solving	irritability	loss of or increase in appetite
weakness	poor abstract thinking	depression	hyper alert to environment
chest pain	poor attention/ decisions	intense anger	increased alcohol consumption
headaches	poor concentration/memory disorientation of time, place or person	apprehension	change in usual communications
elevated BP	difficulty identifying objects or people heightened or lowered alertness	emotional shock	etc...
rapid heart rate	increased or decreased awareness of surroundings	emotional outbursts	
muscle tremors	etc...	feeling overwhelmed	
grinding of teeth		loss of emotional control	
shock symptoms		inappropriate emotional response	
visual difficulties		etc...	
profuse sweating			
difficulty breathing			
etc...			

* Any of these symptoms may indicate the need for medical evaluation. When in doubt, contact a physician

Once you have determined that you or someone you're working with or assisting may be suffering from Critical Incident Stress, please look at and share this information proved on how to help some of these responses.

THINGS TO TRY:

1. Within the first 24-48 hours, periods of strenuous physical exercise.
2. Structure your time—keep busy.
3. You're normal and having normal reactions. Don't label yourself crazy.
4. Talk to people. Talk is the most healing medicine.
5. Be aware of numbing the pain with overuse of drugs or alcohol. You don't need to complicate this with a substance abuse problem.
6. Reach out—people do care.
7. Maintain as normal a schedule as possible.
8. Spend time with others.
9. Help your co-workers as much as possible by sharing feelings and checking out how they are doing.
10. Give yourself permission to feel rotten and share your feeling with others.
11. Keep a journal; write your way through those sleepless hours.
12. Do things that feel good to you.
13. Realize that those around you are under stress.
14. Don't make any big life changes.
15. Do make as many daily decisions as possible which will give you a feeling of control over your life, i.e., if someone asks you what you want to eat—answer them, even if you aren't sure.
16. Get plenty of rest.
17. Recurring thoughts, dreams, or flashbacks are normal—don't try to fight them—they'll decrease over time and become less painful.
18. Eat well-balanced and regular meals (even if you don't feel like it).

FOR FAMILY MEMBERS AND FRIENDS

1. Listen carefully and spend time with the person who is hurting.

2. Offer your assistance and a listening ear even if they have not asked for help.

3. Reassure them that they are safe.

4. Help them with everyday tasks like cleaning, cooking, caring for the family, minding children.

5. Give them some private time.

6. Don't take their anger or other feelings personally.

7. Don't tell them that they are "lucky it wasn't worse"—traumatized people aren't consoled by that. Tell them you're sorry this event has occurred and that you want to understand and help.

Critical incident stress is a very real problem for those working in the emergency response world, both for themselves and those they are serving. It is a fact that the more one sees, the more one may experience a form of critical incident stress. Some of this looks like burn out and post traumatic stress disorder.

Understanding that each and every person dealing with a critical incident in their life may respond in a different way to any type of assistance is very important. When in doubt and most often, it is very beneficial to seek the expert advice of a mental health professional or critical incident specialist before attempting any type of debriefing.

CISD Criticism
A number of studies have shown that CISD (Critical Incident stress Debriefings) has little effect, or that it actually worsens the trauma symptoms. On the other hand, Jacobs, Horne-Moyer and Jones argue that CISM has beneficial effects when conducted with emergency services personnel, but does not work or does more harm than good with accident victims.

There are a couple different models for doing a critical incident stress debriefing. Always use properly trained personnel and follow the guidelines for confidentiality and non-critiquing at all times.

If you or someone you know has experienced a poorly done or disturbing debriefing you will understand the importance of attending one that is run properly and done in a way that benefits the majority of those in attendance.

Please do not attempt to hold a debriefing without a properly trained facilitator to run it.

Chapter Four
Domestic Violence

Domestic violence and abuse can happen to anyone, yet the problem is often overlooked, excused, or denied. This is especially true when the abuse is psychological, rather than physical. Emotional abuse is often minimized, yet it can leave deep and lasting scars.

Noticing and acknowledging the warning signs and symptoms of domestic violence and abuse is the first step to ending it. No one should live in fear of the person they love. If you recognize yourself or someone you know in the following warning signs and descriptions of abuse, don't hesitate to reach out. There is help available.

SIGNS THAT YOU'RE IN AN ABUSIVE RELATIONSHIP

Your Inner Thoughts and Feelings
Do you:

- feel afraid of your partner much of the time?
- avoid certain topics out of fear of angering your partner?
- feel that you can't do anything right for your partner?
- believe that you deserve to be hurt or mistreated?
- wonder if you're the one who is crazy?
- feel emotionally numb or helpless?

Your Partner's Belittling Behavior
Does your partner:

- humiliate or yell at you?
- criticize you and put you down?
- treat you so badly that you're embarrassed for your friends or family to see?
- ignore or put down your opinions or accomplishments?
- blame you for his own abusive behavior?
- see you as property or a sex object, rather than as a person?

Your Partner's Violent Behavior or Threats
Does your partner:

- have a bad and unpredictable temper?
- hurt you, or threaten to hurt or kill you?
- threaten to take your children away or harm them?
- threaten to commit suicide if you leave?
- force you to have sex?
- destroy your belongings?

Your Partner's Controlling Behavior
Does your partner:

- act excessively jealous and possessive?
- control where you go or what you do?
- keep you from seeing your friends or family?
- limit your access to money, the phone, or the car?
- constantly check up on you?

Violent and abusive behavior is the abuser's choice

Despite what many people believe, domestic violence and abuse is not due to the abuser's loss of control over his behavior. In fact, abusive behavior and violence is a deliberate choice made by the abuser in order to control you.

Abusers use a variety of tactics to manipulate you and exert their power:

- **Dominance** – Abusive individuals need to feel in charge of the relationship. They will make decisions for you and the family, tell you what to do, and expect you to obey without question. Your abuser may treat you like a servant, child, or even as his possession.

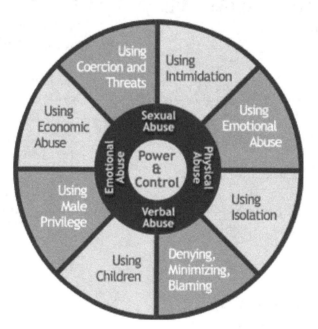

- **Humiliation** – An abuser will do everything he can to make you feel bad about yourself or defective in some way. After all, if you believe you're worthless and that no one else will want you, you're less likely to leave. Insults, name-calling, shaming, and public put-downs are all weapons of abuse designed to erode your self-esteem and make you feel powerless.
- **Isolation** – In order to increase your dependence on him, an abusive partner will cut you off from the outside world. He may keep you from seeing family or friends, or even prevent you from going to work or school. You may have to ask permission to do anything, go anywhere, or see anyone.
- **Threats** – Abusers commonly use threats to keep their partners from leaving or to scare them into dropping charges. Your abuser may threaten to hurt or kill you, your children, other family members, or even pets. He may also threaten to commit suicide, file false charges against you, or report you to child services.

- **Intimidation** – Your abuser may use a variety of intimidation tactics designed to scare you into submission. Such tactics include making threatening looks or gestures, smashing things in front of you, destroying property, hurting your pets, or putting weapons on display. The clear message is that if you don't obey, there will be violent consequences.
- **Denial and blame** – Abusers are very good at making excuses for the inexcusable. They will blame their abusive and violent behavior on a bad childhood, a bad day, and even on the victims of their abuse. Your abusive partner may minimize the abuse or deny that it occurred. He will commonly shift the responsibility on to you: Somehow, his violent and abusive behavior is your fault.

Reasons we know an abuser's behaviors are not about anger and rage:

- He does not batter other individuals - the boss who does not give him time off or the gas station attendant that spills gas down the side of his car. He waits until there are no witnesses and abuses the person he says he loves.
- If you ask an abused woman, "can he stop when the phone rings or the police come to the door?" She will say "yes". Most often when the police show up, he is looking calm, cool and collected and she is the one who may look hysterical. If he were truly "out of control" he would not be able to stop himself when it is to his advantage to do so.
- The abuser very often escalates from pushing and shoving to hitting in places where the bruises and marks will not show. If he were "out of control" or "in a rage" he would not be able to direct or limit where his kicks or punches land.

Source: Mid-Valley Women's Crisis Service

The Full Cycle of Domestic Violence

A man **abuses** his partner. After he hits her, he experiences self-directed **guilt**. He says, "I'm sorry for hurting you." What he does not say is, "Because I might get caught." He then **rationalizes** his behavior by saying that his partner is having an affair with someone. He tells her "If you weren't such a worthless whore I wouldn't have to hit you." He then **acts contrite**, reassuring her that he will not hurt her again. He then **fantasizes** and reflects on past abuse and how he will hurt her again. He **plans** on telling her to go to the store to get some groceries. What he withholds from her is that she has a certain amount of time to do the shopping. When she is held up in traffic and is a few minutes late, he feels completely justified in assaulting her because "you're having an affair with the store clerk." He has just **set her up**.

Source: Mid-Valley Women's Crisis Service

The cycle of violence in domestic abuse

Domestic abuse falls into a common pattern, or cycle of violence:

- **Abuse** – Your abusive partner lashes out with aggressive, belittling, or violent behavior. The abuse is a power play designed to show you "who is boss."
- **Guilt** – After abusing you, your partner feels guilt, but not over what he's done. He's more worried about the possibility of being caught and facing consequences for his abusive behavior.
- **"Normal" behavior** – Your abuser does everything he can to regain control and keep you in the relationship. He may act as if nothing has happened, or he may turn on the charm. This peaceful honeymoon phase may give you hope that your abusive partner has really changed this time.
- **"Normal" behavior** — The abuser does everything he can to regain control and keep the victim in the relationship. He may act as if nothing has happened, or he may turn on the charm. This peaceful honeymoon phase may give the victim hope that the abuser has really changed this time.
- **Fantasy and planning** – Your abuser begins to fantasize about abusing you again. He spends a lot of time thinking about what you've done wrong and how he'll make you pay. Then he makes a plan for turning the fantasy of abuse into reality.
- **Set-up** – Your abuser sets you up and puts his plan in motion, creating a situation where he can justify abusing you.

Your abuser's apologies and loving gestures in between the episodes of abuse can make it difficult to leave. He may make you believe that you are the only person who can help him, that things will be different this time, and that he truly loves you. However, the dangers of staying are very real.

Emotional abuse is when an intimate partner has...

- continually criticized you, called you names or shouted at you
- insulted or driven away your friends or family
- humiliated you in private or public
- kept you from working, controlled your money or made all the decisions
- refused to work or to share money
- taken car keys or money from you
- regularly threatened to leave or told you to leave
- threatened to kidnap the children when the abuser was angry with you
- abused pets to hurt you
- manipulated you with lies and contradictions

Physical abuse is when an intimate partner has...

- pushed or shoved you
- held you to keep you from leaving
- slapped or bitten you
- kicked or choked you
- hit or punched you
- thrown objects at you
- locked you out of the house
- abandoned you in dangerous places
- refused to help you when you were sick, injured or pregnant
- forced you off the road or driven recklessly
- threatened to hurt you with a weapon

Sexual abuse is when an intimate partner has...

- minimized the importance of your feelings about sex
- criticized you sexually
- insisted on unwanted or uncomfortable touching
- withheld sex and affection
- forced sex after physical abuse or when you were sick
- raped you
- been jealously angry, assuming you would have sex with anyone
- insisted that you dress in a more sexual way than you wanted

Long-term effects of domestic violence on women who have been abused may include:

- anxiety
- chronic depression
- chronic pain
- death
- dehydration
- dissociative states
- drug and alcohol dependence
- eating disorders
- emotional "over-reactions" to stimuli
- general emotional numbing
- health problems
- malnutrition
- panic attacks
- poor adherence to medical recommendations
- poverty
- repeated self-injury
- self neglect
- sexual dysfunction
- sleep disorders
- somatization disorders
- strained family relationships
- suicide attempts
- an inability to adequately respond to the needs of their children.

In a 1999 study from Johns Hopkins, it was reported that abused women are at higher risk of miscarriages, stillbirths, and infant deaths, and are more likely to give birth to low birth weight children, a risk factor for neonatal and infant deaths. In addition, children of abused women were more likely to be malnourished and were more likely to have had a recent untreated case of diarrhea and less likely to have been immunized against childhood diseases.

Domestic violence can severely impair a parent's ability to nurture the development of their children. Mothers who are abused may be depressed or preoccupied with the violence. They may be emotionally withdrawn or numb, irritable or have feelings of hopelessness. The result can be a parent who is less emotionally available to their children or unable to care for their children's basic needs. Battering fathers are less affectionate, less available, and less rational in dealing with their children. Studies even suggest that "battered women may use more punitive child-rearing strategies or exhibit aggression toward their children."

When children cannot depend on their parents or caregivers - for emotional support and for practical support - their development can be seriously delayed or, in severe cases, permanently distorted. Children without an emotionally available parent may withdraw from relationships and social activities. Since childhood is the time when social skills and attitudes are learned, domestic violence can affect their ability to form relationships for the rest of their lives.

Parents who have been traumatized by violence must cope with their own trauma before they are able to help their children.

CHILDREN:

According to the American Medical Association, estimates are that more than 3.3 million children are exposed to physical and verbal spousal abuse each year. Exposure means seeing or hearing the actual abuse or dealing with the aftermath of the abuse. When describing the effects of domestic violence on children, it is important to note that domestic violence and child abuse are often present in the same families. "In homes where domestic violence occurs, children are physically abused and neglected at a rate 15 times higher than the national average. Several studies have shown that in 60% to 75% of families in which a woman is battered, children are also battered." In addition, children living in households where domestic violence is occurring are at a higher risk for sexual abuse.

The effects of witnessing or experiencing violence at home vary from one child to another. The attributes that give a child the greatest chance of surviving unscathed are "average or above-average intellectual development with good attention and interpersonal skills. Also feelings of self-esteem and self-efficacy, attractiveness to others in both personality and appearance, individual talents, religious affiliations, socioeconomic advantage, opportunities for good schooling and employment, and contact with people and environments that are positive for development."

Many children in families where domestic violence has occurred appeared to be forced to grow up faster than their peers, often taking on the responsibility of cooking, cleaning and caring for younger children. Laura Gillberg, MSW, is the child and adolescent program director at Sarah's Inn, an agency in Oak Park, Illinois. She stated, "Many of these children were not allowed to have a real childhood. They don't trust their fathers because of his role as an abuser and they may have been worried about what to expect when coming home. They learned at a young age to be prepared for anything."

Children may also be isolated. Typical activities such as having friends over to their house may be impossible due to the chaotic atmosphere.

Kids don't want to have their friends over when mom has a black eye. However, school performance is not always obviously affected. Children may respond by being overachievers.

Gillberg noticed that children in domestic violence tend to be either extremely introverted or extremely extroverted. Psychosomatic problems (aches and pains for no apparent reason) are common; these children's eating and sleeping patterns tend to be disrupted. Children who witness domestic violence can develop behavior problems, including aggression and violent outbursts.

Underlying all these "symptoms" of domestic violence are children's emotional responses: i.e. anger - misery - intense terror - fear of dying - fear of the loss of a parent. Children may feel rage, guilt, or a sense of responsibility for the violence, which can stifle emotional and social development. To learn and grow into a healthy adult, children must feel confident in the world and in themselves. Domestic violence can wipe out a child's confidence and leave them shocked.

INFANTS AND TODDLERS:

Infants and toddlers who witness violence show excessive irritability, immature behavior, sleep disturbances, emotional distress, fears of being alone, and regression in toileting and language. Preschool children may develop enuresis and speech disfluencies, such as stuttering. Exposure to trauma, especially family violence, can interfere with a child's normal development of trust and later exploratory behaviors, which lead to the development of autonomy.

TEENS:

Being a teenager is difficult, as most of us remember. But being a teenager and living in a house infected with domestic violence can have devastating, life-long effects. Teens living with domestic violence face the unique problem of trying to fit in with their peers while keeping their home life a secret. Teens in shelters often face the problem of having to move and begin school in a new place, having to make new friends while feeling the shame of living in a shelter. Needless to say, their family relationships can be strained to the breaking point. The result can be teens that never learn to form trusting, lasting relationships, or teens that end up in violent relationships themselves.

In addition, teens face the same issues as younger children in an abusive family, namely feeling lonely and isolated, growing up too fast, behavior problems, stress related medical and mental health problems, and school problems. Teenagers are also faced with entering into the dating world for the first time. They are formulating their own theories about relationships, and some may not have the best models on which to base a healthy relationship. They have witnessed the cycle of violence with the abuse, apologies from the perpetrator, tensions building and more abuse. Unfortunately, some teenagers may be faced with a higher risk of being victims of dating violence and as mentioned earlier, ending up in violent relationships as adults either as victims or abusers.

Gender trends: Women make up 3/4 of the victims of homicide by an intimate partner. Actually, 33% of all women murdered (of course, only cases which are solved are included) are murdered by an intimate partner. Women make up about 85% of the victims of non-lethal domestic violence. In all, women are victims of intimate partner violence at a rate about 5 times that of males.

Racial and Ethnic trends: Black women and men suffer from the highest rates of domestic violence. Black females experienced domestic violence at a rate 35% higher than that of white females, and about 22 times the rate of women of other races. Black males experienced domestic violence at a rate about 62% higher than that of white males and about 22 times the rate of men of other races.

Age trends: Domestic violence is most prominent among women aged 16 to 24.

Economic Trends: Poorer women experience significantly more domestic violence than higher income women.

Marital status: For both men and women, divorced or separated persons were subjected to the highest rates of intimate partner victimization, followed by never- married persons.

Reporting to police: The rates at which individuals report domestic violence to police vary along racial and gender lines. Hispanic and black women report domestic violence at the highest rate (approximately 65% to 67% of abuse is reported). For white females, only about 50% of the abuse is reported.

Chapter Five

Stalking

Simple Obsessional:
A prior relationship exists between the victim and the stalker which includes the following:
Acquaintance, neighbor, customer, professional relationship, dating, and lover
The stalking behavior begins after either:
The relationship has gone "sour", or
The offending individual perceives some mistreatment
The stalker begins a campaign either to rectify the schism, or to seek some type of retribution

Erotomania:
Based on the Diagnostic Statistical Manual, 4th ed. (<u>DSM-IV, 4th ed.</u>)
The central theme of the delusion is that another person is in love with the individual
The delusion often concerns idealized romantic love and spiritual union rather than sexual attraction — "a perfect match"
The object of affection is usually of a higher status and can be a complete stranger
Efforts to contact the victim are common, but the stalker may keep the delusion a secret
Males, seen most often in forensic samples, come into contact with the law during misguided pursuits to "rescue" the individual from some imagined danger. Females are seen most often in clinical samples

Love Obsessional:
Similar to the erotomanic individuals:
The victim is almost always known through the media.
The delusion that the victim loves them may also be held
The erotomanic delusion is but one of several delusions and psychiatric symptoms — this individual has a primary psychiatric diagnosis
These individuals may be obsessed in their love, without having the belief that the target is in love with them
A campaign is begun to make his/her existence known to the victim

There are several signs that are good indicators of stalking behavior. It is also important to consider the intensity of such behaviors.

1. Persistent phone calls despite being told not to contact in any form.

2. Waiting at workplace or in neighborhood.

3. Threats.

4. Manipulative behavior (for example: threatening to commit suicide in order to get a response to such an "emergency" in the form of contact).

5. Sending written messages: letters, emails, graffiti...

6. Sending gifts from the seemingly "romantic" (flowers and/or candy) to the bizarre (dog teeth, a bed pan, a blood soaked feather) (<u>Dietz et al. 1991b</u>).

7. Defamation: The stalker often lies to others about the victim (claims of infidelity, for example).

8. "Objectification": The stalker derogates the victim, reducing him/her to an object -- this allows the stalker the ability to feel angry with the victim without experiencing empathy (<u>Meloy and Gothard, 1995</u>).

Stalking Behavior Continuum

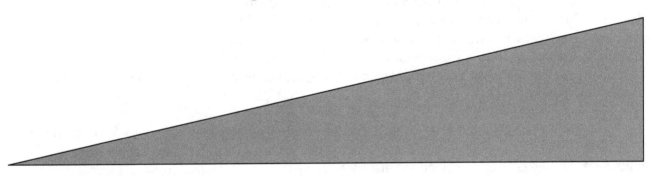

Low intensity, less intrusive,
non-persistent or low
frequency

Inappropriate, problematic,
harassing

Severe in intensity,
persistent, aggressive

Inappropriate,
problematic, harassing

Rethinking What We Tell Our Stalking Victims
Tracy Bahm, Form Director of the Stalking Resource Center

The Stalking Resource Center is always looking for the best, most up-to-date advice to give stalking victims. We subscribe to many journals and newsletters, and we read books on stalking. As we talk to practitioners in the field, we learn more about this crime and what can be done to help keep victims safe. One result of this search is that we are constantly rethinking and reevaluating the criminal justice system's responses to stalking.

Because stalking has been recognized as a crime for only about a decade, our approach to the problem is still in its "infancy." Creative practitioners around the country have come up with some great ways to respond to the crime and to keep victims safe. Those ideas, shared and spread around the country, have gained wide acceptance. For the most part, that's great. But what do we do when we find out that our well-intentioned advice might actually be putting victims in danger? Experts are now struggling to find the best advice for victims about whether, when, and how they should respond to contact from their stalkers.

One common piece of advice is telling victims that if they "just ignore the stalker, the stalking will stop." Experience has taught us that this advice seldom works. The stalker is pursuing the victim for a reason, and the behavior is likely to escalate if he or she is not getting the desired reaction from the victim. For example, if a victim who is being stalked via the Internet completely stops using the computer (even if that were possible), the stalker usually recognizes that he or she is being ignored and does something else to get the victim's attention. Rather than ignoring the behavior, victims of stalking should seek help from trained advocates and law enforcement officers.

We are also reconsidering what to tell victims who report that stalkers are harassing or threatening them by phone. The standard advice has been that victims should disconnect their phones and get a new, unlisted phone number. Getting a new number is a good idea, but it turns out that disconnecting the old one may be a mistake. The Seattle Police Department's Domestic Violence Unit has found that when stalking victims disconnect the phone, virtually 100 percent of the stalkers escalate their contact to in-person stalking. The Seattle Police now advise victims to get a new phone number but keep their old phone line active and connected to an answering machine to capture any possible evidence.

So, if ignoring stalkers doesn't work, what about the advice many well-meaning professionals often give victims, to tell their stalkers-once and forcefully-to leave them alone? This advice may serve a purpose if the stalker doesn't understand that his or her attentions are unwelcome and fear-inducing. Such stalkers may stop if they are appropriately warned. However, much stalking involves unmistakably deliberate behavior that could never be confused with innocent, possibly welcome, non-criminal behavior. In such cases, encouraging a victim to have contact with the stalker, in any form, only increases the stalker's sense of power and control. Even when a warning seems appropriate, a great deal of thought and safety planning must precede contact with the stalker. Trained law enforcement officers or other legal agents, rather than the victim, should deliver the warning (which should not be a substitute for criminal charges). Because stalkers are dangerously unpredictable, warnings can put them "over the edge," further endangering the victim.

So, as you work with victims, please keep helping them with safety planning and threat assessment. Keep looking for better ways to address the problem of stalking. But, as you do, think through the ramifications of all your advice and regularly reevaluate your strategies to make sure they are working as intended. Never underestimate the potential threat that a stalker may pose. And, as you figure out what is effective and what isn't, please share your insights with us, so we can pass them along to other practitioners in the field! Contact us at src@ncvc.org.

In January of 2009, The U.S. Department of Justice released a report based on a national crime victim's survey of stalking and harassment victims. Below are just a few of the statistics of this 16 page report.

- During a 12-month period an estimated 14 in every 1,000 persons age 18 or older were victims of stalking.
- About half (46%) of stalking victims experienced at least one unwanted contact per week,

and 11% of victims said they had been stalked for 5 years or more.
- The risk of stalking victimization was highest for individuals who were divorced or separated—34 per 1,000 individuals.
- Women were at greater risk than men for stalking.
- About 43% of victims stated that police were contacted at least once regarding the stalking.
- Male (37%) and female (41%) stalking victimizations were equally likely to be reported to the
  police.
- Approximately 1 in 4 stalking victims reported some form of cyberstalking such as e-mail (83%) or instant messaging (35%). Electronic monitoring was used to stalk 1 in 13 victims (i.e. GPS
  monitoring, bugs, phone tapping, and video).
- 46% of stalking victims felt fear of not knowing what would happen next.
- Nearly 3 in 4 stalking victims knew their offender in some capacity.

Chapter Six

Sexual Assaults

Sexual assault does not always mean a woman being raped by a stranger that jumps out of the dark woods. While it is true that rape by a stranger is a form of sexual assault, there are also a lot of unwanted sexual contacts that people experience that qualifies as sexual assault. Sexual assault can include child sexual abuse, rape, attempted rape, incest, exhibitionism, voyeurism, obscene phone calls, fondling, and sexual harassment. There is a range of nonconsensual sexual acts that create a continuum in which each form of sexual assault is linked to the others by their root causes, as well as by the effects they have on individuals and communities. While sexual assault can take many forms, it is important to remember that the loss of power and control that a victim of sexual assault experiences is a common thread.

Child sexual abuse can be defined as any situation in which an adult or another child threatens or forces or manipulates a child into sexual activity. Many times the offender doesn't need to use physical force with the victim. Instead, they take advantage of their own position of trust and authority. Child sexual abuse can include exposing a child to pornography, fondling the sexual parts of a child's body, making a child engage in sexual activity with others, and sexually penetrating a child, orally, anally or vaginally with the penis, hand or any object. Incest is intercourse or touching of sexual parts between an adult family member and a child or between siblings.

Rape is any sexual intercourse with a person without his or her consent. It is an act of violence that uses sex as a weapon. There are many different types of rape that are important to distinguish as well. Stranger rape happens when the victim does not know his or her offender. Many people believe that this type of rape only happens to women who dress a certain way, walk alone at night, or park in parking garages. The reality of stranger rape is that it happens during the day and at night, to people from all different walks of life, and in lots of different places.

Acquaintance rape describes a rape in which the victim and the perpetrator are known to each other. The perpetrator might be a partner, coworker, best friend or neighbor. Did you know that this is the most common type of rape? 84 percent of rapes happen among people who know one another. Most of the time a person is raped by someone they know, trust, or love.

Date rape is a specific kind of acquaintance rape, referring to a rape that occurs between two people who are dating partners. Often times the victim is emotionally manipulated or coerced into having sex with his or her partner. Marital rape, one of the least talked about forms of sexual assault, is rape between husband and wife. Because of personal and societal barriers to reporting marital rape, its prevalence is probably higher than we are aware.

Sexual harassment is any unwelcome sexual advances, requests for sexual favors, and other verbal or physical conduct of a sexual nature. Sexual harassment often manifests itself in subtle ways, such as sexually suggestive comments, unwanted touching, risqué jokes, or blatant demand for sexual contact. In most cases, these actions take place within work or educational settings where both the offender and the victim are required to be in close contact.

There are many types of sexual assault. It is important to understand the differences between them, as well as how they are linked together. Unfortunately, because of the silence that surrounds sexual assault, there have been many myths created over time to help explain why it happens and who it happens to. We often hear things like "only women can be raped", "a husband can't rape his wife", "she asked for it by wearing those shorts", and "that child must be lying - his father is a good man." We know that these things are not true. Both women and men can be sexually assaulted. Rape can occur within a marriage. A victim never asks to be raped and is never to blame for behavior of the perpetrator. People who sexually assault are often people who go to church, have good jobs, and are well liked by their community.

Sexual assault involves both sexual behavior and aggression; accordingly, researchers must consider situational influences (i.e., cues) relevant to both behaviors, such as the location or social situation in which the assault occurs. These cues may differ somewhat depending on the type of sexual assault (i.e., stranger sexual assault versus date sexual assault). In the case of sexual assaults that occur among strangers or people who have just met, men who drink heavily may frequent settings, such as bars and parties, where women also tend to drink heavily and where a man can easily find an intoxicated woman to target for a possible sexual assault. In these situations, alcohol may give men the "liquid courage" required to act on their desires and may reinforce their stereotypes about drinking women. For example, an incarcerated rapist interviewed by Scully (1991) stated that, "Straight, I don't have the guts to rape. I could fight a man but not that." (p. 124)

Alcohol consumption is also used by date rapists to excuse their behavior. For example, 62 percent of the college date rapists interviewed by Kanin (1984) felt that they had committed rape because of their alcohol consumption. These rapists did not see themselves as "real criminals," because real criminals used weapons to assault strangers. In fact, some men may purposely get drunk when they want to act sexually aggressive, knowing that intoxication will provide them with an excuse for their socially inappropriate behavior.

As described earlier, at least 80 percent of all sexual assaults occur during social interaction, typically on a date. The fact that sexual assault often happens in situations in which consensual sex is a possible outcome means that a man's interpretation of the situation can influence his responses. Consequently, additional situational factors are relevant to these types of sexual assaults. For example, American men are socialized to be the initiators of sexual interactions. Consequently, if a man is interested in having sex with a woman, he is likely to feel that he should make the first move.

Initial sexual moves are usually subtle in order to reduce the embarrassment associated with potential rejection. Both men and women are used to this indirect form of establishing sexual interest and usually manage to make their intentions clear and save face if the other person is not interested (Abbey et al. 1996b). However, because the cues are subtle and sometimes vague, miscommunication can occur, particularly if communication skills are impaired by alcohol use.

As male-female interaction progresses, a woman who has been misperceived as being interested in sex may realize that her companion is reading more into her friendliness than she intended. However, she may not feel comfortable giving a direct message of sexual disinterest, because traditional female gender roles emphasize the importance of being nice and "letting men down easy." The man, in turn, may not take an indirect approach to expressing sexual disinterest seriously. Research on the power of stereotypes, expectancies, and self-fulfilling prophecies demonstrate that when people have an expectation about a situation or another person, they tend to observe and recall primarily the cues that fit their hypothesis and to minimize or ignore the cues that contradict their hypothesis. Consequently, when a man hopes that a woman is interested in having sex with him, he will pay most attention to the cues that fit his expectation and disregard cues that do not support his expectation. Studies with both perpetrators and victims have confirmed that the man's misperception of the woman's degree of sexual interest is a significant predictor of sexual assault (Abbey et al. 1996a, 1998).

The process just described can occur even in the absence of alcohol use. However, alcohol consumption can exacerbate the likelihood of misperception, thereby increasing the chances of sexual assault. Before describing these dynamics, the laboratory research findings on alcohol's effects on aggressive and sexual behavior should be reviewed.

When working with a sexual assault victim we need to keep in mind the role we play. We are support for the victim in a very quiet way. Once we have gained their trust by just being there it may be ok to ask them if they want to talk or if they need anything else from you. They may be talking non-stop or be very quiet, but they need to set the tone. Letting them know that it's not their fault is a good thing to do and to try and provide any referrals you can think of to get them the help they need. Rape crisis counselors are very beneficial to have in your call out phone book.

As with any other victim you are providing advocacy to, never, ever, tell them your story or say you know how they feel. Even if you are a past victim of the same crime, no two people feel the same and they don't want to hear that right now anyway.

Chapter Seven

Threat Assessments

Threat assessments are a very valuable tool used when determining the level of danger a victim may be in. Whether it is a victim of domestic violence, stalking or work place violence, these threats and all aspects of the subject and victims behavior must come into play when helping to determine safety plans. If we use a tool wisely to help determine ones level of danger, we can help them make a better safety plan. One thing we can NEVER do though is to reassure them that this assessment is a true "prediction" of one's behavior to come. It is impossible to predict what a person will or won't do 100%, it is however determining what might possibly happen because of some of the clues we have, it helps to make a better safety plan and can help the victim become more aware of what might happen if they are not extra careful.

A threat assessment can also help a victim understand the level of danger that isn't there too. Sometimes a victim feels a great fear for reasons that we can't actually detect. This is what we call putting a face on their fear. Once we can determine what it is exactly that they are afraid of then we can deal with each fear individually until the victim feels they have control over it. For example if the victim says I am terrified of my ex-boyfriend! We want to know why. What makes her terrified? What is she afraid he may do? If she is terrified he will slash her tires and say bad things about her and that is the extent of it…well we can deal with that pretty simply! We can put together a safety plan for her that day and help her deal with her fear head-on. There is really no better way to reassure a victim like a good safety plan that works.

Sometimes when a victim says they are terrified of the suspect they are really terrified of losing their lives. A threat assessment that comes back as a high risk is reason enough to do a serious rethinking on a safety plan. Re-location is sometimes the only option but must also be put into place with other safety planning as well. A detailed safety plan MUST come with all threat assessments and they need to be redone if things change. Good follow-up with these victims is essential. They often times need guidance with their plans and reassurance that even though some of the things they have to do seem unfair, they are necessary for their safety. It is never fair that a victim is victimized in the first place and then to tell them they may need to move, frequent other stores and hang outs can all be just too much for some of them to handle.

Gavin DeBecker (author of Gift of Fear) writes that we need to place a value on the threat. This value helps us determine the plausibility of the threat. This judgment is based on a lot of circumstances such as mental health background, employment history, capability, emotional investment, desperation, dedication, frustration and any delusions involving the targeted person.

Assessment of a situation is what a threat assessment means, not assessing a person, this is vital to remember. This is why we must make the victim aware that we are not able to predict behavior from a single person but that we can assess the possibility of a situation that may or may not happen. To do otherwise would be profiling and would cause us to look like failures more often than not if the suspect didn't do exactly what we predicted they would do. This would never help a victim.

Dangerousness is situational and everyone has the potential to be dangerous, so saying that a person we are worried about has that potential is silly! We all do, so we need to see how dangerous the circumstances are, not the person alone. When doing an assessment we have to see the things we cannot change and realize what we can't cure. So we need to reduce the possibility of an encounter by the victim and the threatening person, this will enhance their security and is in our control, their control. We are unable to modify the behavior of the one making the threat, victims need to understand this. A person that has violence in their past may be an indication of how that person deals with problems in their life, however the absence of violence in ones past does not mean that person is not capable of or may be violent in the future.

Is the victim accessible? This is a number one concern, keeping your personal information guarded is a key in minimizing your exposure to the outside world. Watching for pre-incident indicators is what will help us determine what could possibly be a step the threatening person might be able or willing to take. How we respond to the threats is also very important to a safety plan. If the response is not measured against what level of vulnerability the victim has themselves in, there is greater potential for harm to be done. Almost every situation can be managed if the victim is willing to make some changes, some serious changes in their safety. Managing the victims fear is a huge step in this procedure.

If you can manage their fear and make the victim understand they have the power to make certain changes that can make all the difference in their safety and quality of life, then you have won well over half the battle. "It's not fair" is something you hear the victims state over and over as they are told to make changes in their lives to avoid conflict with the threatening person. They may be asked to change locks, change routes to work, get a different car, move out of town and every other thing that is common and usual in their lives. They are right! It's not fair but it's the way for them to help prevent any violence in their lives, they are ultimately responsible for protecting themselves. There is no other person as concerned with or willing to protect the victim as much as the victim themselves. They hold the answers to whether a safety plan will work or fail.

Chapter Eight

Special Populations

WORKING WITH SPECIAL POPULATION GROUPS

MOOD DISORDERS

How much of the population is affected by mood disorders?

Each year, according to the Substance Abuse and Mental Health Administration almost 44 million Americans experience a mental disorder. In fact, mental illnesses are among the most common conditions affecting health today.

What causes mood disorders / mental illness?

Researchers believe most serious mental illnesses are caused by complex imbalances in the brain's chemical activity. They also believe environmental factors can play a part in triggering, or cushioning against, the onset of mental illness.

Are mood disorders treatable?

Like other diseases, mental illnesses can be treated. The good news is that most people who have mental illnesses, even serious ones, can lead productive lives with proper treatment. Mood disorders are one form of serious mental illness.

What are some common mood disorders?

Two of the most common mood disorders are depression and bipolar disorder, also known as manic-depressive illness.

Bipolar Disorder

Description:
Extreme mood swings punctuated by periods of generally even-keeled behavior characterize this disorder. Bipolar disorder tends to run in families. This disorder typically begins in the mid-twenties and continues throughout life. Without treatment, people who have bipolar disorder often go through devastating life events such as marital breakups, job loss, substance abuse, and suicide.

Symptoms:
Mania-expansive or irritable mood, inflated self-esteem, decreased need for sleep; increased energy; racing thoughts; feelings of invulnerability; poor judgment; heightened sex drive; and denial that anything is wrong. Depression-feelings of hopelessness, guilt, worthlessness, or melancholy; fatigue; loss of appetite for food or sex; sleep disturbances, thoughts of

death or suicide; and suicide attempts. Mania and depression may vary in both duration and degree of intensity.

Formal Diagnosis:
Although scientific evidence indicates bipolar disorder is caused by chemical imbalances in the brain, no lab test exists to diagnose the disorder. In fact, this mental illness often goes unrecognized by the person who has it, relatives, friends, or even physicians. The first step of diagnosis is to receive a complete medical evaluation to rule out any other mental or physical disorders. Anyone who has this mental illness should be under the care of a psychiatrist skilled in the diagnosis and treatment of bipolar disorder.

Treatment:
Eighty to ninety percent of people who have bipolar disorder can be treated effectively with medication and psychotherapy. Self-help groups can offer emotional support and assistance in recognizing signs of relapse to avert a full-blown episode of bipolar disorder. The most commonly prescribed medications to treat bipolar disorder are three mood stabilizers: lithium carbonate, carbamazepine, and valproate.

Depression

Description:
When a person's feelings of sadness persist beyond a few weeks, he or she may have depression. According to the National Institute for Mental Health, three to four million men are affected by depression; it affects twice as many women. Researchers do not know the exact mechanisms that trigger depression. Two neurotransmitters-natural substances that allow brain cells to communicate with one another-are implicated in depression: serotonin and norepinephrine.

Symptoms:
Changes in appetite and sleeping patterns; feelings of worthlessness, hopelessness, and inappropriate guilt; loss of interest or pleasure in formerly important activities; fatigue; inability to concentrate; overwhelming sadness; disturbed thinking; physical symptoms such as headaches or stomachaches; and suicidal thoughts or behaviors.

Formal Diagnosis:
Four or more of the previous symptoms have been present continually, or most of the time, for more than 2 weeks. The term clinical depression merely means the episode of depression is serious enough to require treatment. Major depression is marked by far more severe symptoms, such as literally being unable to drag oneself out of bed. Another form of depression, known as seasonal affective disorder, is associated with seasonal changes in the amount of available daylight.

- Each year, depression affects about 17 million American adults; that's almost one in every 10. (American Psychiatric Association, 1998 and National Mental Health Association, 1997)

- Depression can occur at any age but most often appears for the first time between the ages of 24 and 44. (American Psychiatric Association, 1998 and National Depressive & Manic-Depressive Association, 1999)
- One in four women and one in 10 men will confront depression at some point in their lives. (American Psychiatric Association, 1998)
- Two out of three persons suffering from depression do not seek or receive proper treatment. (National Mental Health Association, 1997)
- Eighty to 90% of people who receive treatment for depression show improvement. (American Psychiatric Association, 1998)
- People with severe, untreated depression have an estimated suicide rate of 15 percent. In fact, the number one cause of suicide in the U.S. is untreated depression. (National Depressive & Manic-Depressive Association, 1999)
- Depression costs the U.S. $43 billion annually, when taking into account medical expenses, days missed from work, lost productivity, and premature death. Absenteeism from work alone amounts to $12 billion. (American Psychiatric Association, 1998 and American Psychological Association, 1999)
- Depression will be the second greatest cause of premature death and disability worldwide by the year 2020. (World Health Organization, 1998)

Treatment:
Some types of cognitive/behavioral therapy and interpersonal therapy may be as effective as medications for some people who have depression. Special bright light helps many people who have seasonal affective disorder.

Three major types of medication are used to treat depression: tricyclics; the newer selective serotonin re-uptake inhibitors (SSRIs), and monoamine oxidase inhibitors (MAO inhibitors). Electroconvulsive therapy uses small amounts of electricity applied to the scalp to affect neurotransmitters in the brain.

Usually referred to as ECT, this highly controversial and potentially life-saving technique is considered only when other therapies have failed, when a person is seriously medically ill and/or unable to take medication, or when a person is very likely to commit suicide. Substantial improvements in the equipment, dosing guidelines and anesthesia have significantly reduced the possibility of side effects.

Anxiety Disorders

What are anxiety disorders?

Anxiety disorders range from feelings of uneasiness to immobilizing bouts of terror. This fact sheet briefly describes the different types of anxiety disorders. This fact sheet is not exhaustive, nor does it include the full range of symptoms and treatments. Keep in mind that new research can yield rapid and dramatic changes in our understanding of and approaches to mental disorders. If you believe you or a loved one has an anxiety disorder, seek competent, professional advice or another form of support.

Generalized Anxiety Disorder: Most people experience anxiety at some point in their lives and some nervousness in anticipation of a real situation. However if a person cannot shake unwarranted worries, or if the feelings are jarring to the point of avoiding everyday activities, he or she most likely has an anxiety disorder.

Symptoms: Chronic, exaggerated worry, tension, and irritability that appear to have no cause or are more intense than the situation warrants. Physical signs, such as restlessness, trouble falling or staying asleep, headaches, trembling, twitching, muscle tension, or sweating, often accompany these psychological symptoms.

Formal diagnosis: When someone spends at least six months worried excessively about everyday problems. However, incapacitating or troublesome symptoms warranting treatment may exist for shorter periods of time.

Treatment: Anxiety is among the most common, most treatable mental disorders. Effective treatments include cognitive behavioral therapy, relaxation techniques, and biofeedback to control muscle tension. Medication, most commonly anti-anxiety drugs, such as benzodiazepine and its derivatives, also may be required in some cases. Some commonly prescribed anti-anxiety medications are diazepam, alprazolam, and lorazepam. The non-benzodiazepine anti-anxiety medication buspirone can be helpful for some individuals.

Panic Disorder: People with panic disorder experience white-knuckled, heart-pounding terror that strikes suddenly and without warning. Since they cannot predict when a panic attack will seize them, many people live in persistent worry that another one could overcome them at any moment.

Symptoms: Pounding heart, chest pains, lightheadedness or dizziness, nausea, shortness of breath, shaking or trembling, choking, fear of dying, sweating, feelings of unreality, numbness or tingling, hot flashes or chills, and a feeling of going out of control or going crazy.

Formal Diagnosis: Either four attacks within four weeks or one or more attacks followed by at least a month of persistent fear of having another attack. A minimum of four of the symptoms listed above developed during at least one of the attacks. Most panic attacks last only a few minutes, but they occasionally go on for ten minutes, and, in rare cases, have been known to last for as long as an hour. They can occur at any time, even during sleep.

Treatment: Cognitive behavioral therapy and medications such as high-potency anti-anxiety drugs like alprazolam. Several classes of antidepressants (such as paroxetine, one of the newer selective serotonin reuptake inhibitors) and the older tricyclics and monoamine oxidase inhibitors (MAO inhibitors) are considered "gold standards" for treating panic disorder. Sometimes a combination of therapy and medication is the most effective approach to helping people manage their symptoms. Proper treatment helps 70 to 90 percent of people with panic disorder, usually within six to eight weeks.

Phobias: Most of us steer clear of certain, hazardous things. Phobias however, are irrational fears that lead people to altogether avoid specific things or situations that trigger intense anxiety. Phobias occur in several forms, for example, agoraphobia is the fear of being in any situation that might trigger a panic attack and from which escape might be difficult. Social phobia is a fear of being extremely embarrassed in front of other people. The most common social phobia is fear of public speaking.

Symptoms: Many of the physical symptoms that accompany panic attacks - such as sweating, racing heart, and trembling - also occur with phobias.

Formal Diagnosis: The person experiences extreme anxiety with exposure to the object or

situation; recognizes that his or her fear is excessive or unreasonable; and finds that normal routines, social activities, or relationships are significantly impaired as a result of these fears.
Treatment: Cognitive behavioral therapy has the best track record for helping people overcome most phobic disorders. The goals of this therapy are to desensitize a person to feared situations or to teach a person how to recognize, relax, and cope with anxious thoughts and feelings. Medications, such as anti-anxiety agents or antidepressants, can also help relieve symptoms. Sometimes therapy and medication are combined to treat phobias.

Post-traumatic Stress Disorder: Researchers now know that anyone, even children, can develop PTSD if they have experienced, witnessed, or participated in a traumatic occurrence-especially if the event was life threatening. PTSD can result from terrifying experiences such as rape, kidnapping, natural disasters, or war or serious accidents such as airplane crashes. The psychological damage such incidents cause can interfere with a person's ability to hold a job or to develop intimate relationships with others.
Symptoms: The symptoms of PTSD can range from constantly reliving the event to a general emotional numbing. Persistent anxiety, exaggerated startle reactions, difficulty concentrating, nightmares, and insomnia are common. People with PTSD typically avoid situations that remind them of the traumatic event, because they provoke intense distress or even panic attacks.
Formal Diagnosis: Although the symptoms of PTSD may be an appropriate initial response to a traumatic event, they are considered part of a disorder when they persist beyond three months.
Treatment: Psychotherapy can help people who have PTSD regain a sense of control over their lives. They also may need cognitive behavior therapy to change painful and intrusive patterns of behavior and thought and to learn relaxation techniques. Support from family and friends can help speed recovery and healing. Medications, such as antidepressants and anti-anxiety agents to reduce anxiety, can ease the symptoms of depression and sleep problems. Treatment for PTSD often includes both psychotherapy and medication.

Schizophrenia and other psychotic disorders

What is schizophrenia?

Contrary to the common misconception, schizophrenia does not mean "split or multiple personality." And, although people with schizophrenia often are portrayed as violent on television and in movies, that is seldom the case. Schizophrenia is one of the most disabling and puzzling mental disorders. Just as "cancer" refers to numerous related illnesses, many researchers now consider schizophrenia to be a group of mental disorders rather than a single illness.

How is schizophrenia developed?

Generally, schizophrenia begins in late adolescence or early adulthood. Research indicates a genetic link to the development of schizophrenia. A child who has one parent with schizophrenia, for example, has about a 10 percent chance of developing the illness, compared with a one percent chance if neither parent has schizophrenia. Current research implicates abnormalities in both the brain's structure and biochemical activities. Researchers also tend to agree that environmental influences may be involved in the onset of schizophrenia.

More information about schizophrenia:

Symptoms:
Psychotic, or "positive," symptoms include delusions (bizarre thoughts that have no basis in reality); hallucinations (hearing voices, seeing nonexistent things, and experiencing sensations, such as burning, that have no source); and disordered thinking (apparent from a person's fragmented, disconnected and sometimes nonsensical speech). Other "negative" symptoms include social withdrawal, extreme apathy, diminished motivation, and blunted emotional expression.

Formal Diagnosis:
Active symptoms of the illness (such as a psychotic episode) for at least two weeks, with other symptoms lasting six months.

Treatment: People who have schizophrenia often require medication to control the most troubling symptoms. Antipsychotic medications help bring biochemical imbalances closer to normal. The newer drugs may also be effective for symptoms such as social withdrawal, extreme apathy, and blunted emotional expression. More such drugs are being developed.

Recovery: After these symptoms are controlled, psychotherapy and self-help groups can assist people who have schizophrenia learn to develop social skills, cope with stress, identify early warning signs of relapse, and prolong periods of remission. In addition, support groups and family therapy can give loved ones a better understanding of the illness and help them provide the compassion and support that play an important role in recovery. The good news is that more many of those who have schizophrenia can work, live in the community or with their families, and enjoy friends if they receive continuous, appropriate treatment. According to The National Alliance on Mental Illness, treatment of schizophrenia is successful in 60 percent of patients.
Note: This information is intended only as a starting point for gaining an understanding about schizophrenia. It is by no means exhaustive, nor does it include the full range of symptoms and treatments. Keep in mind that new research can yield rapid and dramatic changes in our understanding of, and approaches to, mental disorders.

WORKING WITH VICTIMS WITH DISABILITIES

Barriers to Services for Victims with Disabilities

There are many reasons why persons with disabilities may not report crime or encounter difficulties in accessing victim services. For example:

- *Communication barriers*: Many criminal justice and victim assistance programs do not have basic access to telecommunication systems (TDD and TTY systems) for deaf victims that facilitate communication, enabling them to more easily report a crime and learn about victim services. Few programs offer victims' rights and services information in Braille or through audio-recorded information so that blind victims can more readily access assistance.

- *Mobility barriers*: Many criminal justice and victim assistance programs have not yet examined the barriers of accessibility to victims in wheelchairs, or to other mobility-impaired crime victims. Special transportation and assistance should be provided for these victims to allow them an opportunity to fully exercise their rights to participate in criminal justice proceedings or to access emergency services, such as a shelter.
- *Dependency issues*: Often, crime victims with disabilities do not report their victimization because it is inflicted upon them by caretakers -- family members or by staff within facilities and institutions designed to assist them. They are dependent on those who abuse them and may be unable to report the crime. Also, victims may have limited communication abilities due to mental impairments and may lack the ability to verbalize their victimization.
- *Isolation and fear*: Many battered women, sexual assault victims, and child victims experience a sense of isolation and fear that they will be blamed for their victimization because of the nature of the victimization and the relation with the perpetrator. These concerns are intensified for victims of these crimes who have disabilities and who are essentially cut off from services due to communication and/or mobility barriers. Moreover, when victims with disabilities are abused by a member of their own "community," these concerns multiply. For example, a deaf battered woman abused by her deaf husband may find that few programs exist within the deaf community to assist her. Turning to the "hearing community," which has little experience with her particular circumstances, for assistance may increase her sense of isolation.

Guidance for Working with Crime Victims with Disabilities

- Look directly at the victim when addressing him/her. Deliberately averting someone's gaze is impolite and can be uncomfortable. Tension is only increased when you avoid eye contact.
- Feel free to ask a victim with a disability how you should act or communicate most effectively with him/her, if you have any doubt about the appropriateness of the situation.
- Address and speak directly to the victim with a disability, even if he/she is accompanied or assisted by a third party.
- Feel free to offer physical assistance to a victim with a disability such as offering your arm if the need arises, but do not assume the victim will need it or accept it.
- Ask a victim with a disability if he/she has any needs that will require special services or arrangements, and then attempt to make arrangements to meet those needs.
- Don't stare at or avoid looking at a visible disability or express sympathy for the victim's disability.
- Don't tell the victim with a disability you admire his/her courage or determination for living with his/her disability. The victim with a disability does not want to be thought of as unusually brave or as a super hero.
- Don't avoid humorous situations which occur as a result of a disability. Take your cue from the victim.

Strategies for Responding to the Needs of Hearing Impaired Victims

- Create a list of referral services for hearing impaired victims. For crisis counseling backup services, check with the State Department of Mental Health, as they usually have specialized counselors available for deaf persons in emergency situations.
- Develop a resource directory of qualified professional (court certified, if possible) interpreters for assistance with hearing impaired victims. Do not rely on friends or family members -- remember, there is no literal translation from English to sign language.
- Have a court-certified interpreter assist you in putting together an informational program brochure for hearing impaired crime victims to ensure that deaf victims will understand the information provided.
- Install a TDD or a TTY telephone to make your program accessible for hearing impaired victims. Training on this equipment is readily available.
- There may be cases in which the victim is a hearing juvenile whose parents are hearing impaired. An interpreter should be secured for communication with these parents in and out of the court. This should be done any time members of the victim's immediate family are hearing impaired.

Tips for Effective Communication with Hearing Impaired Victims

- Directly face a person who is speech reading. Make sure your face is at the victim's eye level. Speak slowly and distinctly, but not unnaturally. Avoid gesturing around the face, since that is distracting during speech reading.
- Avoid having bright or glaring light behind you when addressing a speech reader because the shadows that are cast render your lips invisible.
- If you are eating, chewing, smoking, etc., while talking to a hearing impaired victim, your speech will be much more difficult for the victim to understand.
- Reduce background noises during conversation. Close the office door or turn off any radio, etc., if necessary.
- A sign language interpreter should be properly positioned. He/she should sit next to you so that the hearing impaired victim can shift his/her gaze back and forth from the interpreter to you easily.
- Speak in a normal tone of voice without shouting.
- Do not refer to a deaf person as "deaf and dumb." The ability to speak and/or communicate effectively is unrelated to an individual's ability to hear.
- It is not necessary to avoid using "hear" with a deaf person.
- It is appropriate to tap the hearing impaired person on the shoulder or to wave your hand to get visual contact. Get the hearing impaired person's attention before you start speaking to him/her.
- If a hearing impaired person has obvious difficulty understanding something, find a different way of saying the same thing rather than repeating the original words over and over.

**Strategies for Responding to the Needs of Victims
with Visual Impairments**

There are many different types of visual impairments, and only a small fraction of these individuals are totally blind. Even if a person is determined legally blind, forms and shapes may still be distinguished. The National Victims Center estimates that 80 percent of all visually impaired persons have some remaining vision.

Visually impaired victims face a great deal of mobility problems. A visually impaired victim may need the use of a cane, a guide dog, or a sighted escort. It is essential that service providers recognize the importance of these aides to the victim, and efforts should be made to ensure that the appropriate accommodations are given to the victim. Transportation issues should be discussed to help the visually impaired victim to and from your office or court as necessary. It is also appropriate to allow the visually impaired victim to become acquainted with the physical surroundings of your office, as well as the courtroom if necessary, where he/she may be coming for interviews and/or hearings. Additionally, victim service providers should not assume that a visually impaired person wants a guided escort; rather the victim service provider should extend his/her arm to the victim while asking the victim if he/she wants guidance.

Tips for Effective Communication with Visually Impaired Victims

- Whenever a visually impaired person enters your office, immediately indicate your presence verbally, approach him/her, and give your name.
- When speaking to a visually impaired person, use a normal tone and pace your speech patterns; it is not necessary to speak louder. Do not stop talking when a blind person is approaching you because he/she relies on the sound of your voice for direction.
- Speak directly to a visually impaired victim, not to a third party who may accompany the victim.
- When a blind person enters your office, it may be helpful to extend your arm to take and guide the victim to a chair. Then, place his/her hand on the back of the chair and tell the victim whether "the chair has arms" in order to direct the victim as he/she sits down.
- If there are other individuals in your office, a blind person may be unaware of this. Introduce each person by name and indicate where they are sitting in the room relative to where the blind person is seated.
- If you must leave the visually impaired person's presence for some reason, tell him/her you are leaving for awhile.
- It is not necessary to avoid using the words "see," "look," or "blind" with a visually impaired person because he/she is used to these words also.
- When giving visually impaired persons directions, be as clear and specific as possible. Make sure to identify obstacles in the direct path of travel. Since some visually impaired persons have no visual memory (having been blind since birth), be careful of using descriptions containing numbers of feet or yards, rather use the number of steps for a distance measure. If you are unsure of just how to direct a visually impaired person, say something like, "I would be happy to give you directions. How should I describe things?"

Effectively Responding to the Needs of Mobility Impaired Victims

The National Victim Center estimates that approximately six percent of the population has some form of mobility impairment. The disability is generally a result of congenital defects, diseases, accidents, military combat, or injuries received during a crime. Numerous physical conditions may result in mobility impairment. Some examples would include: spinal cord injuries; cerebral palsy; muscular dystrophy; epilepsy; or, a combination of these conditions.

There are generally two types of barriers that persons with mobility impairments have in society: architectural and attitudinal. Examples of architectural barriers include stairways, doors that are too narrow to accommodate wheelchairs, sidewalk curbs, and an insufficient number of handicapped parking spaces. Attitudinal barriers are usually more subtle. Examples include, but are not limited to, reactions of disgust, pity, or discomfort expressed verbally and non-verbally.

Strategies for Responding to the Needs of Mobility Impaired Victims

- Do not assume that the mobility impaired victim needs your assistance. An individual in a wheelchair or with a walker or braces will not normally require your help entering a room.
- Provide mobility assistance only if you are asked.
- Service providers should be aware that victims with mobility impairments may have difficulty opening doors, manipulating objects, may need special equipment, and help in getting from one place to another.
- Be aware that a person's wheelchair is a part of his/her body space and needs to be treated as such. Do not stand too close to the wheelchair, as this could block the mobility impaired victim's movement with the wheelchair if they wanted or needed to move about.
- One of the primary concerns in any case involving a mobility impaired victim or witness will be accessibility to the courthouse and other criminal justice system offices and facilities when necessary. Arrange for transportation to and from your office or the courtroom, if needed. Ask specific questions concerning the mobility impaired victim's travel needs so that you can arrange for the proper transportation prior to the time it will be required.
- Be aware of the location of wheelchair ramps and accessible restrooms so that you can direct the victim to these facilities, if needed.

**Tips for Effective Service Delivery for Victims
with Speech Impairments**

- Do not assume that a person with a speech impairment is intellectually impaired. There is no inherent connection between the two.
- Relax while listening. Your ear will adjust more quickly to the sound of the victim's speech.
- If you cannot understand the speech impaired victim's comment or response to a question, ask him/her to repeat what he/she has said. If you are still unable to discern what is being said, you might consider asking the speech impaired victim to write it out for you.
- You may lose valuable information if you do not follow up on answers or comments that are confusing or that do not make sense to you

TRIBAL CONCERNS

Isolation and alienation Tribal members have a unique culture that is characterized by being exclusive. Members of the tribe tend to look down on those who look outside of their culture for help. This is an obstacle that can be overcome through compassion and continued work in the community.

Jurisdictional boundaries The tribes operate under their own legal systems. These systems are federal and tend to circumvent local jurisdictions. This can be extremely confusing. The best battle plan for this obstacle is learning specifics about the tribal justice system and getting to no tribal council members.

Transportation Issues Many members of the tribes do not have basic transportation. This particular issue is generally easy to overcome in that the tribes requests a letter explaining the situation and the need for travel. A voucher is then given from the tribe to the tribe member for a variety of different things

Substance abuse and chronic unemployment Alcohol abuse is a continuing and serious problem in American Indian communities, said Gordon Belcourt, the council's executive director."Part of the problem is people are using alcohol and drugs to escape," Belcourt said. The future can seem grim to young American Indians living on reservations with high rates of unemployment and substance abuse, he said. As many as 13 percent of American Indians are dependent on alcohol, according to the council's statistics. That is more than three times the rate of alcoholism in the general population.

WORKING WITH RURAL POPULATIONS

The biggest obstacles to rural populations are as follows. The fewer people you have, the fewer resources you have. One of the biggest things to combat this problem is the number of resources that exist specifically for rural programs. There are STOP grants that aim specifically at the crimes of domestic and sexual abuse. There are specific grants for rural programs under the Violence against Women Act and the Victims of Crime Act. The best clearing house for these grants can be found that the Office for Victims Of Crime web site. The National Grange of the Order of Patrons of Husbandry gives grants to rural communities for many different purposes. You also need to think locally as many local businesses see giving to victim services as a positive advertisement.

WORKING WITH CAMPUS CRIME VICTIMS

Obstacles you may encounter with campus crime are that there is a general perception of a lack of services available at campus facilities. This generally is a lack of perception and not an actual lack of services. One way to check is to see what services are available in your local campus before you have a need for those services.

Peer pressure also becomes an obstacle in that campuses are small compacted communities. Everyone knows your name. There is an inherent feeling that if someone reports a crime everyone will know about it. One way to get around this is to have interviews and services provided at a location separate from the campus.

There has been a lack of understanding about the expertise campus security offices have. This is a knowledge problem and is best fought by fact. Local law enforcement can help combat this mis-perception by including campus security officers in their training and accepting training offered by the campus security officers.

WORKING WITH HOMOSEXUAL-LESBIAN-OTHER GENDERED VICTIMS

There is a massive amount of under-reporting in crimes involving homosexual, lesbian and other gendered victims. This is for several cultural and survival reasons. One of the biggest fears from this community is that the victim will be "outed". Outing is when a person's sexual preference is exposed to the general public. This community is an isolated group. Whenever a group is isolated you will have underreporting and a lack of access to basic services.

Depending on the community you live in there may be an extreme lack of understanding regarding the issues in the homosexual, lesbian or other gendered community.

Working well with this community is extremely important because you may get only one shot at helping these victims. Respecting them the same as all other victims is essential.

WORKING WITH AFRICAN AMERICAN, HISPANIC and NATIVE AMERICAN VICTIMS

There can be a lack of understanding of cultural barriers. There is a long history of discrimination involving minorities. There can, and usually are issues of mistrust with law enforcement. One way to combat this mistrust is to explain the steps in the process and express what is typically done in each case. This is something we do with every victim. The goal when dealing with victims of any type of race, gender, or ability is to offer services to them all and deliver them in a consistent manner.

WORKING WITH INTOXICATED VICTIMS

Intoxicated victims can be very difficult to work with. For this reason law enforcement often will not call Victim Services to a scene due to the intoxication level of the victim. The key thing to remember when working with intoxicated victims is safety. Remember intoxicated victims have the following issues:
- They have difficulty processing information
- They can have wildly varying mood swings
- They can become violent at the drop of a hat

For these reasons keep the information you are giving to the intoxicated victim unusually simple. You may want to give them your contact information, get there contact information, and simply contact them at a later date.

DO NOT MEET WITH INTOXICATED VICTIMS ALONE!!

WORKING WITH HOMICIDE SURVIVORS

One of the biggest questions homicide survivors need an answer to is the question of why. For this reason homicide family members will feel a need to know every detail. This will mean that the victim will feel the need to ask for updates on a daily basis. The homicide survivor generally feels that their personal security has been threatened. They will have a high need to feel safe.

A good strategy to work with the homicide survivor is to pick one day of the week to be an update day. This will allow for the survivor to look to that day to process their questions and will allow you as the victim service provider to work other cases and still stay on top with your homicide survivor. You may want to address personal safety right from the beginning by address the status of the suspect as well as general personal safety rules.

Remember that all homicide cases are large media events. Instruct your homicide survivor that they do not have to talk to the media. **Check with the investigating agency to get approval of what can be released before releasing any information.**

WORKING WITH THE NEEDY VICTIM

Some victims, for a variety of reasons, have an unusually high service need. These victims typically have unrealistic expectations about what can and cannot be done for them. These victims also are self focused to the point of not being able to see their own situation clearly.

One good game plan is to set up a contact management plan. This establishes ground rules for contact from the beginning. These victims specifically need to be informed several steps through the process of what can and will be done. Don't tell this victim that you have other victims to service because they will not grasp that and will read into it that you don't care about their case.

If you tell this victim that you will do something for them then you need to follow through with that. On the other hand if you leave a blanket statement like, "If there is anything else I can do for you just call me." Then you have set an unrealistic expectation. You can only do certain things for the victims you serve, don't throw out those blanket feel good statements even though you mean well. It's quite possibly the worst expectation you can provide your victims.

WORKING WITH THE OBSTINATE VICTIM

The old adage that you can lead a horse to water but you can't make him drink is never truer than for the obstinate victim. These victims tend to not follow through on management plans and will make elaborate excuses for doing so. These victims will often appear to have a lot of knowledge about the criminal justice system and may tell you things that you should be doing to manage their case.

Be prepared to remind the obstinate victim that you are giving them tools for their use and that you as a victim services provider cannot use the tools for them. Explain your role in the case clearly and fall back on that explanation throughout the case. Sometimes you will have the victim that starts blaming you or your agency for not helping them more, not doing enough. When this happens and you know that you have provided all of the assistance you could have, reiterate that the victim's safety is ultimately their own responsibility. If they don't follow the safety plan or refuse to make an effort to not stay or become a victim then your hands are tied. This can be a very difficult discussion to have but it is your responsibility to have that discussion.

We see Victim Service providers every year in a burn out phase due to feeling the stress of this type of situation. If you can remember that you are the person handing out ideas and tools and possibly money or a bed for a time, you can stop taking it so personally. The onus is on the victim to make the changes and not you.

WORKING WITH ELDERLY VICTIMS

Elderly victims can be some of the most rewarding victim to work with. An important thing to remember when working with an elderly victim is that they may have a cultural perspective that is different from your own. Many elderly victims lived the majority of their lives without the technological advances we now enjoy. Remember that when asking them for text message evidence and computer evidence. Elderly victims can be quite resourceful with technology and might be offended if you automatically assume they don't know what you're talking about. In the same token, be careful, however, in assuming they will know how to use new technology.

Elderly victim often have a fear of the loss of their freedom. This is something that can come up throughout the case. The elderly victim may have difficulty recollecting specific events and may get frustrated in trying to do so. It is important to tell the elderly victim what your role is and reassure them that you are going to offer tools to protect them. Remember that not all elderly victims are hearing impaired! Don't make the mistake that they can't hear you and start raising your voice unless they ask you too or it appears they can't hear you.

Chapter Nine

Victimology

Victimology is the scientific study of victimization, including the relationships between victims and offenders, the interactions between victims and the criminal justice system — that is, the police and courts, and corrections officials — and the connections between victims and other social groups and institutions, such as the media, businesses, and social movements. Victimology is however not restricted to the study of victims of crime alone but may cater to other forms of human rights violations that are not necessarily crime.

In criminology and criminal law, a victim of a crime is an identifiable person who has been harmed individually and directly by the perpetrator, rather than merely the society as a whole. However, this may not always be the case, as with victims of white collar crime, who may not be clearly identifiable or directly linked to the crime. Victims of white collar crime are often denied their status as victims by the social construction of the concept (Croall, 2001). Not all criminologists accept the concept of victimization or victimology. It also remains a controversial topic within women's studies.

The United States Supreme Court first recognized the rights of crime victims to make a victim impact statement in the sentencing phase of a criminal trial in the case of *Payne v. Tennessee* 501 U.S. 808 (1991).

A victim impact panel is a form of community-based or restorative justice in which the crime victims (or relatives and friends of deceased crime victims) meet with the defendant after conviction to tell the convict about how the criminal activity affected them, in the hope of rehabilitation or deterrence

Consequences of crimes

Emotional distress as the result of crime is a recurring theme for all victims of crime. The most common problem, affecting three quarters of victims, were psychological problems, including: fear, anxiety, nervousness, self-blame, anger, shame, and difficulty sleeping. These problems often result in the development of chronic PTSD (post-traumatic stress disorder). Post crime distress is also linked to pre-existing emotional problems and sociodemographic variables. This has known to become a leading case of the elderly to be more adversely affected.

Victims may experience the following psychological reactions:

- Increase in the belief of personal vulnerability.
- The perception of the world as meaningless and incomprehensible.
- The view of themselves in a negative light.

The experience of victimization may result in an increasing fear of the victim of the crime, and the spread of fear in the community.

Victimization

One of the most controversial sub-topics within the broader topic is victimization. The concept of "victim-proneness" is a "highly moralistic way of assigning guilt" to the *victim of a crime*, also known as victim blaming. One theory, the *environmental theory*, posits that the location and context of the crime gets the victim of the crime and the perpetrator of that crime together. That may just be an academic way of stating that the victim and the perpetrator were in the wrong place at the wrong time.

There have been some studies recently to quantify the real existence of victim-proneness. Contrary to the urban legend that more women are repeat victims, and thus more victim-prone than men, actually men in their prime (24 to 34 year old males) are more likely to be victims of repeated crimes. While each study used different methodology, their results must be taken seriously and further studies are warranted.

The study of victimology may also include the "culture of victimhood," wherein the victim of a crime revels in his status, proclaiming that self-created victimhood throughout a community by winning the sympathy of professionals and peers.

In the case of juvenile offenders, the study results also show that people are more likely to be victimized as a result of a serious offense by someone they know; the most frequent crimes committed by adolescents towards someone they know were sexual assault, common assault, and homicide. Adolescents victimizing people they did not know generally committed common assault, forcible confinement, armed robbery, and robbery.

Examples

One particularly well known example of a class at increased risk to varying forms of attacks is the prostitute. These people have been known anecdotally to have an abnormally high incidence of violent crime, and such crimes go unresolved frequently. Victimological studies of the matter might investigate current societal mores (expectations, roles, social status), legal status of prostitutes, typical working/living conditions, statistical analysis of the actual increased risk and secondary risk factors, and the economic activity of a prostitute.

Another example is when the victim actively precipitates or initiates the crime scene, for example, by starting a fight or baiting another individual.

Victim Facilitation

Victim facilitation, another controversial sub-topic, but a more accepted theory than victim blaming, finds its roots in the writings of criminologists Marvin Wolfgang. The choice to use victim facilitation as opposed to "victim blaming" or some other term is that victim facilitation is not blaming the victim, but rather the interactions of the victim that make he/she vulnerable to a crime.

While victim facilitation relates to "victim blaming" the idea behind victim facilitation is to study the elements that make a victim more accessible or vulnerable to an attack. In an article that summarizes the major movements in victimology internationally, Schneider expresses victim facilitation as a model that ultimately describes only the misinterpretation of victim behavior of the offender. It is based upon the theory of a symbolic interaction and does not alleviate the offender of his/her exclusive responsibility.

In Eric Hickey's *Serial Murderers and their Victims'*, a major analysis of 329 serial killers in America is conducted. As part of Hickey's analysis, he categorized victims as high, low, or mixed regarding the victim's facilitation of the murder. Categorization was based upon lifestyle risk (example, amount of time spent interacting with strangers), type of employment, and their location at the time of the killing (example, bar, home or place of business). Hickey found that 13-15% of victims had high facilitation, 60-64% of victims had low facilitation and 23-25% of victims had a combination of high and low facilitation. Hickey also noted that among serial killer victims after 1975, one in five victims placed themselves at risk either by hitchhiking, working as a prostitute or involving themselves in situations in which they often came into contact with strangers.

There is importance in studying and understanding victim facilitation as well as continuing to research it as a sub-topic of victimization. For instance, a study of victim facilitation increases public awareness, leads to more research on victim-offender relationship, and advances theoretical etiologies of violent crime. One of the ultimate purposes of this type of knowledge is to inform the public and increase awareness so less people become victims.

Another goal of studying victim facilitation, as stated by Godwin, is to aid in investigations. Godwin discusses the theory of victim social networks as a concept in which one looks at the areas of highest risk for victimization from a serial killer. This can be connected to victim facilitation because the victim social networks are the locations in which the victim is most vulnerable to the serial killer. Using this process, investigators can create a profile of places where the serial killer and victim both frequent.

VICTIMOLOGY THEORY

The concept of *victim* dates back to ancient cultures and civilizations, such as the ancient Hebrews. Its original meaning was rooted in the idea of sacrifice or scapegoat -- the execution or casting out of a person or animal to satisfy a deity or hierarchy. Over the centuries, the word *victim* came to have additional meanings. During the founding of victimology in the 1940s, victimologists such as Mendelson, Von Hentig, and Wolfgang tended to use textbook or dictionary definitions of victims as hapless dupes who instigated their own victimizations. This notion of "victim precipitation" was vigorously attacked by feminists in the 1980s, and was replaced by the notion of victims as anyone caught up in an asymmetric relationship or situation. "Asymmetry" means anything unbalanced, exploitative, parasitical, oppressive, and destructive, alienating, or having inherent suffering. In this view, victimology is all about power differentials. Today, the concept of victim includes any person who experiences injury, loss, or hardship due to any cause. Also today, the word *victim* is used rather indiscriminately; e.g., cancer victims, holocaust victims, accident victims, victims of injustice, hurricane victims, crime victims, and others. The thing that all these usages have in common is an image of someone who has suffered injury and harm by forces beyond his or her control.

The term "crime victim" generally refers to any person, group, or entity who has suffered injury or loss due to illegal activity. The harm can be physical, psychological, or economic. The legal definition of "victim" typically includes the following:

- A person who has suffered direct, or threatened, physical, emotional or pecuniary harm as a result of the commission of a crime; or in the case of a victim being an institutional entity, any of the same harms by an individual or authorized representative of another entity. Group harms are normally covered under civil and constitutional law, with "hate crime" being an emerging criminal law development, although criminal law tends to treat all cases as individualized.

Besides "primary crime victims", there are also "secondary crime victims" who experience the harm second hand, such as intimate partners or significant others of rape victims or children of a battered woman. It may also make sense to talk about "tertiary crime victims" who experience the harm vicariously, such as through media accounts or from watching television.

Many victims feel that defining themselves as a "victim" has negative connotations, and choose instead to define themselves as a "survivor." This is a very personal choice that can only be made by the person victimized. The term "survivor" has multiple meanings; e.g. survivor of a crime, "survivor benefits." It remains to be seen whether this terminology for victims of crime will endure.

"Victim defenses" have recently emerged in cases of parricide (killing one's parents) and homicide of batterers by abused spouses. Advocates for battered women were among the first to recognize the issue, and promote the "battered woman syndrome" to defend women who killed or seriously injured a spouse or partner after enduring years of physical, emotional and/or sexual abuse. Attorneys have also drawn upon theories of Post-traumatic Stress Disorder to defend their client's behavior. From time to time, media attention to these defenses becomes intense, and certain "high profile" cases tend to influence public opinion and spread confusion over who is the "victim" and who is the "victimizer." One of the goals of victimology as a science is to help end this state of societal confusion.

The Study of Victimology

Before we can understand victimology, we need to appreciate that it is a fairly new subfield or area of specialization within criminology. Criminology is a rather broad field of study that encompasses the study of law making, law breaking, and societal reactions to law breaking. Victimology, much like criminal justice, falls into the third of these areas. Victimology doesn't have any subfields within itself; in fact, there are few theories, and little or no schools of thought. Going back to criminology, there are four subfields: penology (and the sociology of law); delinquency (sometimes referred to as psychological criminology); comparative (and historical) criminology; and victimology.

Andrew Karmen, who wrote a text on victimology entitled *Crime Victims: An Introduction to Victimology* in 1990, broadly defined victimology:

"The scientific study of victimization, including the relationships between victims and offenders, the interactions between victims and the criminal justice system -- that is, the police and courts, and corrections officials -- and the connections between victims and other societal groups and institutions, such as the media, businesses, and social movements."

From this definition, we can see that victimology encompasses the study of:

- victimization
- victim-offender relationships
- victim-criminal justice system relationships
- victims and the media
- victims and the costs of crime
- victims and social movements

Victimologists often use surveys of large numbers of people about the crimes that have been committed against them because official police statistics are known to be incomplete. Data derived from victimization surveys are carried out each year by the Census Bureau on behalf of the Department of Justice (the NCVS - National Crime Victimization Survey). Victimologists then estimate victimization rates and risks, and do a whole lot more.

If there is any such thing as a method to victimology, here it is:

1. Define the problem - find the asymmetry, analyze responsibility, explore the kinds of harm
2. Measure true dimension of the problem - analyze statistics, see what kind of people are involved, accurately gauge extent of harm
3. Investigate how CJ system handles the problem - look at what CJ system ignores, ask what victim wants, analyze effects, chronicle emergence of victim's movement
4. Examine societal response to problem - look at issues of constitutional rights, analyze proposed legislation, analyze media reaction, see if anyone is cashing in on the problem

History of Victimology

At first (going back to the origins of criminology in the 1880s), anything resembling victimology was simply the study of crime from the perspective of the victim. With the exception of some psychological profilers who do this, nobody really advocates this approach to victimology anymore. The scientific study of victimology can be traced back to the 1940s and 1950s. Two criminologists, Mendelsohn and Von Hentig, began to explore the field of victimology by creating "typologies". They are considered the "fathers of the study of victimology."

These new "victimologists" began to study the behaviors and vulnerabilities of victims, such as the resistance of rape victims and characteristics of the types of people who were victims of crime, especially murder victims. Mendelsohn (1937) interviewed victims to obtain information, and his analysis led him to believe that most victims had an "unconscious aptitude for being victimized."

He created a typology of six (6) types of victims, with only the first type, the *innocent*, portrayed as just being in the wrong place at the wrong time. The other five types all contributed somehow to their own injury, and represented *victim precipitation*.

Von Hentig (1948) studied victims of homicide, and said that the most likely type of victim is the "depressive type" who is an easy target, careless and unsuspecting. The "greedy type" is easily duped because his or her motivation for easy gain lowers his or her natural tendency to be suspicious. The "wanton type" is particularly vulnerable to stresses that occur at a given period of time in the life cycle, such as juvenile victims. The "tormentor," is the victim of attack from the target of his or her abuse, such as with battered women.

Von Hentig's work provided the foundation for analysis of victim-precipitation that is still somewhat evident in the literature today. Wolfgang's research (1958) followed this lead and later theorized that "many victim-precipitated homicides were, in fact, caused by the unconscious desire of the victims to commit suicide." Schafer's theoretical work (1968) also represented how victimology invested a substantial amount of its energy to the study of how victims contribute - knowingly or unknowingly -- to their own victimization, and potential ways they may share responsibility with offenders for specific crimes. In fact, Schafer's book, *The Victim and His Criminal*, from this approach, is supposed to be a corrective to Von Hentig's book, *The Criminal and His Victim*.

Theories in Victimology

Over the years, ideas about victim precipitation have come to be perceived as a negative thing; "victim blaming" it is called. Research into ways in which victims "contribute" to their own victimization is considered by victims and victim advocates as both unacceptable and destructive. Yet a few enduring models and near-theories exist. I'll mention two or three of them:

1. Luckenbill's (1977) Situated Transaction Model - This one is commonly found in sociology of deviance textbooks. The idea is that at the interpersonal level, crime and victimization is a contest of character. The stages go like this: (1) insult - "Your Momma"; (2) clarification - "Whaddya say about my Mother"; (3) retaliation - "I said your Momma and you too"; (4) counter retaliation - "Well, you're worse than my Momma"; (5) presence of weapon - or search for a weapon or clenching of fists; (6) onlookers - presence of audience helps escalate the situation.

2. Benjamin & Master's Threefold Model - This one is found in a variety of criminological studies, from prison riots to strain theories. The idea is that conditions that support crime can be classified into three general categories: (1) precipitating factors - time, space, being in the wrong place at the wrong time; (2) attracting factors - choices, options, lifestyles (the sociological expression "lifestyle" refers to daily routine activities as well as special events one engages in on a predictable basis); (3) predisposing factors - all the sociodemographic characteristics of victims, being male, being young, being poor, being a minority, living in squalor, being single, being unemployed.

3. Cohen & Felson's (1979) Routine Activities Theory - This one is quite popular among victimologists today who are anxious to test the theory. Briefly, it says that crime occurs whenever three conditions come together: (1) suitable targets - and we'll always have suitable targets as long

as we have poverty; (2) motivated offenders - and we'll always have motivated offenders since victimology, unlike deterministic criminology, assumes anyone will try to get away with something if they can; and (3) absence of guardians - the problem is that there's few defensible spaces (natural surveillance areas) and in the absence of private security, the government can't do the job alone.

The phenomena that criminals and victims often have the same sociodemographic characteristics (e.g., are in relatively the same age group) is known as the propinquity hypothesis; and that criminals and victims often live in physical proximity to one another is called the proximity hypothesis.

Societal Influences

America's "law-and-order" movement has continued to overlap with the movement to enhance the legal standing and improve treatment of crime victims. Criminal justice reformers seeking greater accountability for offenders through tougher sentencing have found allies in outspoken violent crime victims and politicians who recognized the public's concern about crime and its impact. The combination has brought greater political support for crime victims' rights legislation and increased funding for crime victim services. Since about 1981 (the start of Victims Rights Week), there has been numerous legislation, conferences, and task forces. Some so-called victim's rights (such as denial of bail, anti-suppression of evidence, and victim-initiated appeals) clearly are anti-defendant and pro-prosecutor to the extent that they undermine cherished principles that an accused person is considered innocent until proven guilty, and that the burden of proof falls on the state.

INTERNET RESOURCES:
Theoretical Perspectives of Victimology

Last updated: 06/19/03

Chapter Ten

Educating our Victims

Victim blaming. We mentioned this in chapter 9, maybe you have even took part in it or defended someone that had it happen to them. It's a very complex subject, however, when we talk here about educating our victims we may almost sound as if we are victim blaming when the fact is we are trying to help victims make safer choices for their future, not blaming them for anything.

I remember when I was a young girl growing up with my older sister. We used to ride our bikes all over the place. We loved to ride and especially loved to fly down any hills we could find. We had limits though, set by those mean old parents that wanted to make sure we stayed in a safe area that wasn't too far from the house. I remember the day we decided to extend our boundaries so we could try the hill we coveted just a few blocks farther down the street. It was exhilarating! We were flying for sure! It was too good to not do it again and we pushed our luck a couple more times. Then it happened. My sister's bike went ripping down that perfect hill and crashed at the bottom, flinging her into a heap a few feet away. I knew it was bad when I saw her face, she was holding her arm funny and couldn't lift her shoulder.

We struggled to push the bike home and she was miserable, crying and in terrible pain. A long story short, she had broken her collar bone, almost broke her neck. She was a victim of her own stupidity is what my Dad told her. Of course they found out where we had been, people talk and we finally confessed too. We took a chance, broke the rules, made a bad decision and it ended up poorly. We were in serious trouble, my sister's broken collar bone was the least of her worries, we were grounded, had our favorite things taken away from us and spent a ton of time doing nothing fun!

I am now the mother of three kids and I teach them also that we make choices in life that are good and bad and some of those choices may cause us to become victims of our own actions. I am a firm believer in the victim's rights movement. I am a victim advocate, coordinator for victim services and a community educator on the subjects of victimology, assessing threats and crime prevention. However, I find the whole victim culpability discussions have taken a turn in a very wrong direction.

I have had numerous classes, speakers and people involved in the business tell me that we can't blame the victims of "certain" crimes even when they have made some very bad and often illegal choices to become a victim. I grew up in a society that made us be responsible for our own actions and then as I matured and understood this ideal, the world took a super liberal swing and started blaming other people for the actions of those that couldn't make good choices for themselves.

Bars were getting sued for drunk drivers crashing their cars, tobacco companies were getting sued for some guy smoking for 60 years and dying of cancer. Victims that put themselves in bad places, don't think about personal safety, make poor choices in what they are doing or who they are hanging out with, need to be educated on what their level of culpability is. If my sister wouldn't have ridden her bike past the end of the block, she may not have broken her collar bone!

My Mother would have locked me in a room till I was 30 years old before she let me wear inappropriate clothing to school, she said it was a bad choice to make and would lead to people miss judging me and I could end up in a predicament I didn't actually invite. I don't think it's a smart idea to advise our future (our children) that we don't care what they do, what choices they make, good, bad, or otherwise, they won't be accountable for anything that happens to them. Because they will. Because they can suffer great harm if they don't pay attention. This is not victim blaming its education of the way the world responds.

Let's take the action of making a safety plan for our victims into consideration in all of this. Will we make a plan that is so sensitive to what this victim was already doing with their life that we ignore huge potential for more danger if we don't advise change? Most effective safety plans are born out of a necessity for a change for safety. We wear seatbelts because to not do so anymore is very STUPID! Studies done prove that seat belts save lives. Drinking and driving is not only very STUPID but it is also illegal and not safe at all! To do so would be certainly putting yourself and possibly others in danger. Wearing a $5,000.00 watch to a basketball game in some crappy crime infested neighborhood might be viewed as the same form of stupidity to most of us! We make choices everyday that may or may not effect what happens to us.

I would dress in a business suit with professional shoes and carry a brief case to a job interview in a professional office building; I wouldn't wear a bikini and flip flops! I think that may affect what happens to me. I bet I wouldn't get the job! I also would not wear a bathrobe to a wedding of a close friend or a party dress to a funeral. If you were to smoke a little weed and then decide to go for a walk with a stranger to get some alcohol and party with them, you might have had some very poor judgment in doing that.

When we think of educating our victims we show them ways to prevent attention from those that might want to harm them. During threat assessment training I had through the UCLA in California I learned what a purse snatcher looks for in an airport. It's not the strong assured woman that's dressed like a professional and has her belongings attached to her closely as she walks with her head up and makes eye contact with those around her. The snatcher is looking for the weak woman, head down purse loosely draped over her shoulder or sitting on her luggage. She may be small in stature but more importantly she appears to be insecure, not confidant or has a physical handicap that may prohibit her from challenging the offender. This is not unlike the victim of an assault or a sexual assault. Many easy targets are often looked at first.

We need to teach our victims how to be less of a target. Domestic violence victims that have taken the big step of getting out of a bad situation are easy targets not only because of their beliefs and uncertainty about being without this person but because this person is also no stranger to the victim. The perpetrator knows everything about the victim as well as all about those that she is related to or friends with, so getting away is often the hardest thing this victim can accomplish. However there are patterns and habits that can be changed, relocation and other extreme measures might have to take place if the safety level is seriously in need of taking care of.

We don't ever want to blame a victim for becoming a victim, they did not "cause" another person to act the way they did. However, educating them to make safer choices is very important to helping them protect themselves.

Domestic Violence Safety Plan

SAFETY AT HOME

Develop a safety plan and discuss it with your children. Review the plan as often as possible. Change the locks and install devices to secure your windows. Make sure your children's school, day-care center, or camp, know who is authorized to pick up your children. Tell your neighbors and landlord that your abuser no longer lives there and ask them to call the police if they see him or her near your home. Before you resume a potentially abusive relationship, discuss alternatives with someone you trust.

SAFETY IN PUBLIC OR AT WORK

If you have an order of protection, keep it with you at all times. Inform building security and coworkers you trust of your situation. If possible, provide a photograph of your abuser to building security. Vary your routes to and from work and arrange for someone to escort you to your car, bus, or train. Plan what to do in various situations if the abuser confronts you.

SAFETY DURING VOLATILE DOMESTIC VIOLENCE INCIDENT

If an argument seems unavoidable, move to a room or area with easy access to an exit - not a bathroom, kitchen, or anywhere near weapons. Identify which door, window, stairwell or elevator offers the quickest way out of the home - and practice your route. Have a bag packed and ready. Keep it in an undisclosed but accessible place where you can retrieve it quickly.

Find neighbors you can tell about the violence and ask that they call the police if they hear a disturbance. Devise a code word to use with your children, family, and friends when you need the police. Decide where you will go if you have to leave, even if you do not think it will come to that.

Use your instincts and judgment. Consider giving the abuser what he or she wants to defuse a dangerous situation. You have a right to protect yourself when you are in danger. You do not deserve to be battered or threatened.

PERSONALIZED SAFETY PLAN

The following steps represent my plan for increasing my safety and preparing in advance for the possibility for further violence. Although I do not have control over my partner's violence, I do have a choice about how to respond to him/her and how to best get myself and my children to safety.

Step 1: SAFETY DURING A VIOLENT INCIDENT. Women cannot always avoid violent incidents. In order to increase safety, battered women may use a variety of strategies.

I can use some or all of the following strategies:

A. If I decide to leave, I will _____. (Practice how to get out safely. What doors, windows, elevators, stairwells or fire escapes would you use?)

B. I can keep my purse and car keys ready and put them _____ _____ (place) in order to leave quickly.

C. I can tell _____ about the violence and request they call the police if they hear suspicious noises coming from my house.

D. I can teach my children how to use the telephone to contact the police and the fire department.

E. I will use _____ as my code for my children or my friends so they can call for help.

F. If I have to leave my home, I will go _____ _____ (Decide this even if you don't think there will be a next time). If I cannot go to the location above, then I can go to _____ or _____ .

G. I can also teach some of these strategies to some/all of my children.

H. When I expect we are going to have an argument, I will try to move to a space that is lowest risk, such as _____ _____. (Try to avoid arguments in the bathroom, garage, and kitchen, near weapons or in rooms without access to an outside door).

I. I will use my judgment and intuition. If the situation is very serious, I can give my partner what he/she wants to calm him/her down. I have to protect myself until I/we are out of danger.

Step 2: SAFETY WHEN PREPARING TO LEAVE. Battered women frequently leave the residence they share with the battering partner. Leaving must be done with a careful plan in order to increase safety. Batterers often strike back when they believe that a battered woman is leaving the relationship.

I can use some or all the following safety strategies:

A. I will leave money and an extra set of keys with_____ so that I can leave quickly.

B. I will keep copies of important papers and documents or an extra set of keys at _____ .

C. I will open a savings account by _____, to increase my independence.

D. Other things I can do to increase my independence include:

E. The domestic violence program's hot line telephone number is _____
and I can seek shelter by calling this hot line.

F. I can keep change for phone calls on me at all times. I understand that if I use my telephone credit card, the following month the telephone bill will tell my batterer those numbers that I called after I left. To keep my telephone communications confidential, I must either use coins or I might get a friend to permit me to use their telephone credit card for a limited time when I first leave.

G. I will check with _____ and
_____ to see who would be able to let me stay with them or lend me some money in an emergency.

H. I can leave extra clothes with_____.

I. I will sit down and review my safety plan every _____ in order to plan the safest way to leave the residence.

_____ (domestic violence advocate or friend) has agreed to help me review this plan.

J. I will rehearse my escape plan and, as appropriate, practice it with my children.

Step 3: SAFETY IN MY OWN RESIDENCE. There are many things that a woman can do to increase her safety in her own residence. It may be impossible to do everything at once, but safety measures can be added step by step.

Safety measures I can use include:

A. I can change the locks on my doors and windows as soon as possible.

B. I can replace wooden doors with steel/metal doors.

C. I can install security systems including additional locks, window bars, poles to wedge against doors, an electronic system, etc.

D. I can purchase rope ladders to be used for escape from second floor windows.

E. I can install smoke detectors and purchase fire extinguishers for each floor in my house/apartment.

F. I can install an outside lighting system that lights up when a person is coming close to my house.

G. I will teach my children how to use the telephone to make a collect call to me and to _____ (friend/minister/other) in the event that my partner takes the children.

H. I will tell people who take care of my children which people have permission to pick up my children and that my partner is not permitted to do so. The people I will inform about pick-up permission include:

_____ (school),

_____ (day care staff),

_____ (babysitter),

_____ (Sunday School teacher),

_____ (teacher),

_____ (and),

_____ (others),

I. I can inform _____, and
_____ (neighbors), _____ (pastor),
and,_____ (friend) that my partner no longer resides with me and they should call the police if he is observed near my residence.

I can find out my risks with Rate Your Risk Tests.

Step 4: SAFETY WITH AN ORDER OF PROTECTION. Many battered women obey protection orders, but one can never be sure which violent partner will obey and which will violate protection orders. I recognize that I may need to ask the police and the court to enforce my protection order.

The following are some steps that I can take to help the enforcement of my protection order:

A. I will keep my protection order_____ (location) (Always keep it on or near your person. If you change a purse, that's the first thing that should go in).

B. I will give my protection order to police departments in the communities where I usually visit family or friends, and in the community where I live.

C. The County Sheriff's Office is the county registry of protection orders that all police departments can call to confirm a protection order. I can check to make sure that my order is in registry. The telephone number for the county registry of protection order is

_____.

D. For further safety, if I often visit other counties in Indiana, I might file my protection order with the court in those counties.

E. I can call the local domestic violence program if I have questions or if I have some problem with my protection order.

F. I will inform my employer, my minister, my closest friend, my relatives, and
_____and
_____that I have a protection order in effect.

G. If my partner destroys my protection order, I can get another copy from the County Courthouse by going to the Circuit Court Clerk's Office, or by contacting the Domestic Violence Unit of the County Prosecuting Attorney.

H. If my partner violates the protection order, I can call the police and report a violation, contact my attorney, call my advocate, and/or advise the court of the violation.

I. If the police do no help, I can contact my advocate or attorney and will file a complaint with the chief of the police department, or Sheriff.

J. I can also file a private criminal complaint with the Prosecuting Attorney in the jurisdiction where the violation occurred. I can request that charges be filed against my battering partner for violation of the Protective Order and all the crimes that he commits in violating the order. I can call the domestic violence advocate for help.

Step 5: SAFETY ON THE JOB AND IN PUBLIC. Each battered woman must decide if and when she will tell others that her partner has battered her and that she may be at continued risk. Friends, family and co-workers can help to protect women. Each woman should consider carefully which people to invite to help secure her safety.

I might do any or all of the following:

A. I can inform my boss, the security supervisor and_____ at work of my situation.

B. I can ask _____ to help screen my telephone calls at work.

C. When leaving work, I can _____.

D. When driving home if problems occur, I can _____.

E. If I use public transit, I can _____.

F. I will go to different grocery stores and shopping malls to conduct my business and shop at hours that are different than those when residing with my battered partner.

G. I can use a different bank and take care of my banking at hours different from those I used when residing with my battered partner.

H. I can also_____.

Step 6: SAFETY AND DRUG OR ALCOHOL USE. Most people in this culture use alcohol. Many use mood-altering drugs. Much of this use is legal and some is not. The legal outcomes of using illegal drugs can be very hard on a battered woman, may hurt her relationship with her children and put her at a disadvantage in other legal actions with her battering partner. Therefore, women should carefully consider the potential cost of the use of illegal drugs. But beyond this, the use of any alcohol or other drug can reduce a woman's awareness and ability to act quickly to protect herself from her battering partner. Furthermore, the use of alcohol or other drugs by the batterer may give him/her an excuse to use violence. Therefore, in the context of drug or alcohol use, a woman needs to make specific safety plans.

If drug or alcohol use has occurred in my relationship with the battering partner, I can enhance my safety by some or all of the following:

A. If I am going to use, I can do so in a safe place and with people who understand the risk of violence and are committed to my safety.

B. I can also_____.

C. If my partner is using, I can_____.

D. I might also_____.

E. To safeguard my children, I might _____

and _____.

Step 7: SAFETY AND MY EMOTIONAL HEALTH. The experience of being battered and verbally degraded by partners is usually exhausting and emotionally draining. The process of building a new life for myself takes much courage and incredible energy.

To conserve my emotional energy and resources and to avoid hard emotional times, I can do some of the following:

A. If I feel down and ready to return to a potentially abusive situation, I can

_____.

B. When I have to communicate with my partner in person or by telephone, I can

_____.

C. I can try to use "I can . . . " statements with myself and to be assertive with others.

D. I can tell myself -"_____

_____" whenever I feel others are trying to control or abuse me.

E. I can read _____ to help me feel stronger.

F. I can call _____, _____and _____as other resources to be of support of me.

G. Other things I can do to help me feel stronger are_____ _____, and_____.

H. I can attend workshops and support groups at the domestic violence program or _____, or _____to gain support and strengthen my relationships with other people.

Step 8: Items to take when leaving. When women leave partners, it is important to take certain items with them. Beyond this, women sometimes give an extra copy of papers and an extra set of clothing to a friend just in case they have to leave quickly.

Money : Even if I have never worked, I may be entitled to the funds in the checking and savings accounts. If I don't take any money from the accounts, he can legally take all money and/or close the account and I may not get my share until the court rules on it if ever.

Items with asterisks on the following list are the most important to take. If there is time, the other items might be taken, or stored outside the home. These items might be placed in one location, so that if we have to leave in a hurry, I can grab them quickly.

When I leave, I should have:

Identification for myself
Children's birth certificate
My birth certificate
Social security cards
School and vaccination records
Money

Checkbook, ATM (Automatic Tellers Machine) card, Credit cards
Keys - house/car/office
Driver's license and registration
Medication
Welfare identification, work permits, Green Card, Passport, divorce papers
Medical records - for all family members
Lease/rental agreement, house deed, mortgage payment book
Bank books, Insurance papers
Small saleable objects
Address book, pictures, jewelry
Children's favorite toys and/or blankets
Items of special sentimental value

Important Numbers You May Need

Emergency-911
Police Department: _____
Sheriff's Office: _____
Police Victim Services: _____
County Sheriffs Victim Services: _____
District Attorney's Office- _____

Work number_____
Supervisor's home number_____
Minister_____
Other_____

I will keep this document in a safe place and out of the reach of my potential attacker.

Review date:_____

IF YOU NEED HELP IN FILLING OUT THIS PLAN YOU MAY ASK POLICE DETECTIVES, COUNSELORS, SHELTER WORKERS, THE SELF HELP CENTER, OR A CLOSE AND TRUSTED FRIEND.

Chapter Eleven

Suicide

The Beginning of the End; Working with Suicidal Subjects and their Loved Ones

You've made your arrangements to take call for your scheduled time. You've picked up the radio and are mentally prepared for your time on call. The phone rings and the dispatch center gives you an address and tells you to respond to the scene of a 16 year old who appears to have shot himself. Now what?

Unfortunately the above described scenario is not uncommon. No matter what the age of the person who has ended his or her life these are not easy calls. This chapter is meant specifically to give you tools to help manage these calls. Remember from the beginning there are several questions you will need to ask the person asking you to respond. The main questions from the beginning are these: 1. Who will you be meeting with? 2. How many people are on scene with the officer(s)? 3. Do we know if the person who found the deceased is still on scene? 4. Has the coroner's office already been dispatched and if so are they already on scene. 5. What is the name of the deceased? The reasons for these questions are profound. The biggest difficulty is that the dispatcher calling you to the scene is not going to know most of the answers to these questions. That is why is so important to communicate directly with the officer in charge of the scene as soon as you get there. Remember that this call could quickly turn into a death notification case. If so remember the keys to death notification located in the chapter on that subject in this book,(chapter 14).

Risk Factors for Suicide

What we know about suicide through decades of study tells us that there are many indicators that point to a higher likelihood for completed suicides. These risk factors are important to look at for you as a first responder. These are important things to look for in those cases where you are dealing with a suicidal subject who has not yet completed the suicide. These risk factors are also important for the loved ones and support network you are dealing with. This also includes first responders.

Age

Elderly and adolescent individuals are at a significantly higher risk for suicide than any other age groups. This is for a number of various reasons. This can be for a number of different reasons. Elderly people tend to have more life altering ailments than younger people. Elderly people also tend to have compiled a greater number of life traumas. Adolescents are growing and tend to be developing their emotional responses to traumas. Because adolescents have a relatively small pool of history to draw from to help in their decision making process they tend to have an all or nothing type of response to everyday traumas. Men over 85 comprise the riskiest gender and age specific category. Suicide is the 3rd leading cause of death in persons between the ages of 15 and 24.

Sex

Studies indicate that women attempt suicide more frequently than men while 72 % of men commit all suicides.

Alcohol Dependence

Alcohol and drugs in general tend to have differing reactions in people depending on a variety of factors including their age, level and history of use, weight, mental status. The key thing is dependence, especially alcohol dependence. Alcohol dependence tends to be a key factor in suicides and suicide attempts. This is one of the many reasons you as a first responder need to express serious concerns about family members and support group members using alcohol to "help" them through after a completed suicide. Alcohol dependent individuals have a 50% higher suicide rate than non alcoholics

Previous Suicide Attempts

In many cases, when talking with family member, you will see a long and storied history of previous suicide attempts in completed suicide cases. In many cases suicidal subjects seem to be investigating what works and what does not. In some cases the suicidal subject will test what works and eventually go too far and complete a suicide.

Short Time Frame Since Last Attempt

If it is within a three month time period since the last suicide attempt there is a high likelihood of a completed suicide.

Depression and Social Isolation

The key here is that depression coupled with social isolation is an almost guaranteed mix for a completed suicide. The key for the first responder is to help to build a social network if one is not readily available. Millions of Americans suffer from depression. Most will not resort to suicide.

Hopeless Feelings

Most studies indicate that the person who feels as though there is no hope will be at a high risk for suicide.

Family History and Organized Plan

Family history is a huge indicator of suicide attempts or future attempt. It is not uncommon to see families that have had generations of suicides in their families. One of the biggest risk factors with completed suicides are organized plans. If someone has thought enough to come up with a plan they need to be especially taken seriously.

Access to Weapons

Completed suicides are 5 times higher in households with firearms. Firearms are more prevalent in suicides involving alcohol.

Taken all of these things into account it is imperative to assess the folks we come into contact with on scenes. **You are not called out because dispatch has nothing better to do!!** We are called out because either a critical incident exists or someone is in enough emotional distress to require our services. What better time to learn how to do a risk assessment.

Suicide Risk Assessment SADPERSONS

Sex
Age
Depression
Previous suicide attempts
Ethanol Abuse
Rational Thinking Loss (psychosis)
Social support stinks
Organized Plan to Complete Suicide
No Spouse (divorced,widowed,single)
Sickness (physical illness)

Assessing the Suicidal Person

It's important to note that on any call you respond to you could be talking with a suicidal person. Remember that **your personal safety is job number 1!** It's hard to help someone if you are disabled and a suicidal subject by their very nature is volatile. DO NOT put yourself in a position in which you are the only person with the possible suicidal subject.

Be empathetic! It cannot be overstated enough that when talking to someone who is suicidal staying open minded is important. This is not always easy. You may have to force yourself to put your beliefs in your pocket temporarily. Remember that your goal is to get the subject to help as soon as possible.

Ask Open Ended Questions. You want to ask questions that force an emotional-thought provoking process. This will allow you to have a better grasp on what is actually going on inside your subjects head. Avoid asking questions that can be automatically responded to with a yes or no answer. The only exception to this is the next question:

Don't be afraid to ask the hard question! Ask if the person is they are thinking about killing themselves. You will not push someone to kill themselves by asking this question. It is a question that needs to be asked.

Did they seek help prior to the attempt? You need to be able to gage if the person has decided in their mind that their life is over or if they are asking for help. Studies indicate that between 50-67%

of completed suicides saw a doctor less than 1 month prior to committing suicide.

How potentially lethal was the attempt? We have met with folks who have tried to take their lives by overdosing on Mylanta.

Access to weapons. Remember that more access the suicidal subject has to kill themselves, the greater the potential for success in the future.

Access to medications. Does the person have access to medications they can overdose with and do they have psychotropic drugs they need to function with.

Myths

There are several myths floating around about suicide. Despite years of published studies to the contrary the following myths are still popular and are still quoted as fact.

1. *Someone who talks about killing themselves won't.* This myth sees its origin in the belief that if someone is talking about killing themselves they really want help. Therefore when someone talks about killing themselves it is a cry for help they will not kill themselves. The difficulty with this myth is that it causes first responders to take down their guard on suicidal subject calls. There is not one fact to back up this myth. In fact studies do indicate that many, although not all, completed suicides were completed by people who had given warning either written or spoken prior to the suicide.
2. *People who try suicide are crazy.* This one has been soundly debunked by any number of studies. The fact that this myth has existed as long as it has speaks to the general lack of knowledge regarding mental health issues.
3. *If someone really wants to die nothing will stop them.* This grows from the understanding that people can and will sometimes go to extraordinary lengths to complete suicide. The facts are early and constant intervention can and does save lives.
4. *Anyone who kills themselves did not want help.* This is an interesting statement in that there is no real way to know what is inside a deceased persons head at the time of their demise. We can go back, however, and look at this person's life prior to the suicide. What we do find is that the vast majority of completed suicides gave several warning flags and in fact voiced their suicidal ideations many times prior to death.
5. *Talking about suicide will give them the idea.* This is simply an off shoot of the taboo nature of the subject of suicide. There is not one study to indicate that someone committed suicide specifically because a first responded asked them if they were going to kill themselves.

Working with Families

Remember that families having experienced a suicide are going through a critical incident. Families and support people will have adrenaline as well as a lot of information going through their systems. **Go slow with questions.** Allow the support system to make the pace with which you give information. **Be prepared.** Gather as much information as you can out of earshot of the family and support people. **Don't dwell on questions about pre-incident indicators.** Now is not the time for psychological autopsy. Your goal as a first responder is simply to give the family and support people information and tools to put their life back together. **Ask questions about when the last good day the love one had.**

You are trying to lead the family back to the path of good memories. This can sometimes be the most difficult part of the call DON'T GIVE UP! **Look for good hooks!!** Look for anything that can connect you emotionally with the family members or support group this will help them to work forward in their grief. Remember not to relay stories about any other suicide. **Prepare them for investigators.** Tell the family and support system that investigators will have a lot of questions. Tell the family what the role of the investigators is and tell the family of the different agencies that will be involved. **Remember support groups but don't nag!** Get a feel for where the family is at emotionally. Never repeat support group information if the family doesn't ask for the information after you have already given it. **You're on their time.** Clear your schedule and remember that this is not a race. If your find yourself looking at your watch several times other than to give other first responders and family time information take your watch off. **This is their loved one!!** We don't have the right to tell others how they should grieve. Remember that playing the blame game will be a natural stress reaction and a big part of the grieving process. Don't step on toes by telling people they shouldn't feel a certain way.

It's sometimes very hard to be present while witnessing extreme anger, guilt and unbelief from the survivors. Being quiet and listening is often all you can do. Allowing them to vent, yell, cry and scream is ok. Just make sure they are not going to hurt themselves doing so or anyone else. On occasion you may find that someone in the survivor mix is blaming another survivor for the suicide. This is a good time to separate these folks if at all possible, you can't tell anyone to feel a different way at this time and this is also a time that the situation can become all about everyone's safety.

Chapter Twelve

Criminal Justice System & Progress of a criminal case

ARREST
The police take the defendant into custody by legal authority because they have reasonable cause to believe they were involved in a crime.

ARRAIGNMENT
After the defendant is booked, informal charges will be filed within a certain period of time (usually between two to 48 hours) following an arrest.

PRELIMINARY HEARING
During this appearance before the judge, bail will be set (with some exceptions). A bail bond is posted as a promise to appear at all subsequent court dates. Failure to appear can result in a bench warrant order for their arrest.

GRAND JURY
If the case occurs on the federal level, a grand jury will decide if there is enough evidence to formally charge the defendant.

INDICTMENT
This is the formal arraignment during which the official charges are read and defendant is asked how they will plea.

PLEA
The defendant has three choices of how they can plea:

Guilty	Not Guilty	NOLO CONTENDERE
Possible plea bargain	Case goes to trial	(No Contest) Possible plea bargain

PRETRIAL
Not guilty pleas send the case to trial. Before the trial, if the defendant requests a jury trial, jury selection will begin. Evidence issues will also be determined before the trial.

TRIAL
The prosecutor has the burden of proof to show the defendant is guilty of the charges in question. The jury will determine the verdict:

ACQUITTAL or CONVICTION

SENTENCING

For "guilty" pleas, "no contest" pleas, and trial convictions, the judge will determine the sentence. In some special circumstances, the jury may influence this decision.

APPEALS

If you feel you did not receive a fair trial and are not satisfied with the results of your trial, you have the legal right to file an appeal with the appropriate court.

THE CHALLENGE OF CRIME IN A FREE SOCIETY

A Report By The President's Commission
On Law Enforcement and Administration of Justice

February 1967

AMERICA'S SYSTEM OF CRIMINAL JUSTICE

The system of criminal justice America uses to deal with those crimes it cannot prevent and those criminals it cannot deter is not a monolithic, or even a consistent, system. It was not designed or built in one piece at one time. Its philosophic core is that a person may be punished by the Government if, and only if, it has been proved by an impartial and deliberate process that he has violated a specific law. Around that core layer upon layer of institutions and procedures, some carefully constructed and some improvised, some inspired by principle and some by expediency, have accumulated. Parts of the system magistrates' courts, trial by jury, bail are of great antiquity.

Other parts juvenile courts, probation and parole, professional policemen are relatively new. The entire system represents an adaptation of the English common law to America's peculiar structure of government, which allows each local community to construct institutions that fill its special needs. Every village, town, county, city, and State has its own criminal justice system, and there is a Federal one as well. All of them operate somewhat alike. No two of them operate precisely alike.

Any criminal justice system is an apparatus society uses to enforce the standards of conduct necessary to protect individuals and the community. It operates by apprehending, prosecuting, convicting, and sentencing those members of the community who violate the basic rules of group existence. The action taken against lawbreakers is designed to serve three purposes beyond the immediately punitive one. It removes dangerous people from the community; it deters others from criminal behavior; and it gives society an opportunity to attempt to transform lawbreakers into law-abiding citizens.

What most significantly distinguishes the system of one country from that of another is the extent and the form of the protection it offers individuals in the process of determining guilt and imposing punishment. Our system of justice deliberately sacrifices much in efficiency and even in effectiveness in order to preserve local autonomy and to protect the individual. Sometimes it may seem to sacrifice too much. For example, the American system was not designed with Cosa Nostra-type criminal organizations in mind, and it has been notably unsuccessful to date in preventing such organizations from preying on society.

The criminal justice system has three separately organized parts the police, the courts, and corrections and each has distinct tasks. However, these parts are by no means independent of each other. What each one does and how it does it has a direct effect on the work of the others. The courts must deal, and can only deal, with those whom the police arrest; the business of corrections is with those delivered to it by the courts. How successfully corrections reforms convicts determines whether they will once again become police business and influences the sentences the judges pass; police activities are subject to court scrutiny and are often determined by court decisions. And so reforming or reorganizing any part or procedure of the system changes other parts or procedures. Furthermore, the criminal process, the method by which the system deals with individual cases, is not a hodgepodge of random actions. It is rather a continuum an orderly progression of events some of which, like arrest and trial, are highly visible and some of which, though of great importance, occur out of public view. A study of the system must begin by examining it as a whole.

The popular, or even the law book, theory of everyday criminal process oversimplifies in some respects and over-complicates in others what usually happens.

That theory is that when an infraction of the law occurs, a policeman finds, if he can, the probable offender, arrests him and brings him promptly before a magistrate. If the offense is minor, the magistrate disposes of it forthwith; if it is serious, he holds the defendant for further action and admits him to bail. The case then is turned over to a prosecuting attorney who charges the defendant with a specific statutory crime. This charge is subject to review by a judge at a preliminary hearing of the evidence and in many places if the offense charged is a felony, by a grand jury that can dismiss the charge, or affirm it by delivering it to a judge in the form of an indictment. If the defendant pleads "not guilty" to the charge he comes to trial; the facts of his care are marshaled by prosecuting and defense attorneys and presented, under the supervision of a judge, through witnesses, to a jury. If the jury finds the defendant guilty, he is sentenced by the judge to a term in prison, where a systematic attempt to convert him into a law-abiding citizen is made, or to a term of probation, under which he is permitted to live in the community as long as he behaves himself.

Some cases do precede much like that, especially those involving offenses that are generally considered "major": serious acts of violence or thefts of large amounts of property. However, not all major cases follow this course, and, in any event, the bulk of the daily business of the criminal justice system consists of offenses that are not major of breaches of the peace, crimes of vice, petty thefts, assaults arising from domestic or street-corner or barroom disputes. These and most other cases are disposed of in much less formal and much less deliberate ways.

The theory of the juvenile court is that it is a "helping" social agency, designed to prescribe carefully individualized treatment to young people in trouble, and that its procedures are therefore non-adversary. Here again there is, in most places, a considerable difference between theory and practice. Many juvenile proceedings are no more individualized and no more therapeutic than adult ones.

What has evidently happened is that the transformation of America from a relatively relaxed rural society into a tumultuous urban one has presented the criminal justice system in the cities with a volume of cases too large to handle by traditional methods. One result of heavy caseloads is highly visible in city courts, which process many cases with excessive haste and many others with excessive slowness. In the interest of both of effectiveness and of fairness to individuals, justice should be swift and certain; too often in city courts today it is, instead, hasty or faltering. Invisibly, the pressure of numbers has effected a series of adventitious changes in the criminal process. Informal shortcuts have been used. The decision making process has often become routinized. Throughout the system the importance of individual judgment and discretion, as distinguished from stated rules and procedures, has increased. In effect, much decision making is being done on an administrative rather than on a judicial basis. Thus, an examination of how the criminal justice system works and a consideration of the changes needed to make it more effective and fair must focus on the extent to which invisible, administrative procedures depart from visible, traditional ones, and on the desirability of that departure.

THE POLICE

At the very beginning of the process or, more properly, before the process begins at all something happens that is scarcely discussed in law books and is seldom recognized by the public: law enforcement policy is made by the policeman. For policemen cannot and do not arrest all the offenders they encounter. It is doubtful that they arrest most of them. A criminal code, in practice, is not a set of specific instructions to policemen but a more or less rough map of the territory in which policemen work. How an individual policeman moves around that territory depends largely on his personal discretion.

That a policeman's duties compel him to exercise personal discretion many times every day is evident. Crime does not look the same on the street as it does in a legislative chamber. How much noise or profanity makes conduct "disorderly" within the meaning of the law? When must a quarrel be treated as a criminal assault: at the first threat or at the first shove or at the first blow, or after blood is drawn, or when a serious injury is inflicted? How suspicious must conduct be before there is "probable cause," the constitutional basis for an arrest? Every policeman, however complete or sketchy his education, is an interpreter of the law.

Every policeman, too, is an arbiter of social values, for he meets situation after situation in which invoking criminal sanctions is a questionable line of action. It is obvious that a boy throwing rocks at a school's windows is committing the statutory offense of vandalism, but it is often not at all obvious whether a policeman will better serve the interests of the community and of the boy by taking the boy home to his parents or by arresting him. Who are the boy's parents? Can they control him? Is he a frequent offender who has responded badly to leniency? Is vandalism so epidemic in the neighborhood that he should be made a cautionary example? With juveniles especially, the police exercise great discretion.

Finally, the manner in which a policeman works is influenced by practical matters: the legal strength of the available evidence, the willingness of victims to press charges and of witnesses to testify, the temper of the community, the time and information at the policeman's disposal. Much is at stake in how the policeman exercises this discretion. If he judges conduct not suspicious enough to justify intervention, the chance to prevent a robbery, rape, or murder may be lost. If he overestimates the seriousness of a situation or his actions are controlled by panic or prejudice, he may hurt or kill someone unnecessarily. His actions may even touch off a riot.

THE MAGISTRATE

In direct contrast to the policeman, the magistrate before whom a suspect is first brought usually exercises less discretion than the law allows him. He is entitled to inquire into the facts of the case, into whether there are grounds for holding the accused.

He seldom does. He seldom can. The more promptly an arrested suspect is brought into magistrate's court, the less likelihood there is that much information about the arrest other than the arresting officer's statement will be available to the magistrate. Moreover many magistrates, especially in big cities, have such congested calendars that it is almost impossible for them to subject any case but an extraordinary one to prolonged scrutiny.

In practice the most important things, by far, that a magistrate does are to set the amount of a defendant's bail and in some jurisdictions to appoint counsel. Too seldom does either action get the careful attention it deserves. In many cases the magistrate accepts a waiver of counsel without insuring that the suspect knows the significance of legal representation.

Bail is a device to free an untried defendant and at the same time make sure he appears for trial. That is the sole stated legal purpose in America. The Eighth Amendment to the Constitution declares that it must not be "excessive." Appellate courts have declared that not just the seriousness of the charge against the defendant, but the suspect's personal, family, and employment situation, as they bear on the likelihood of his appearance, must be weighed before the amount of his bail is fixed. Yet more magistrates than not set bail according to standard rates: so and so many dollars for such and such an offense.

The persistence of money bail can best be explained not by its stated purpose but by the belief of police, prosecutors, and courts that the best way to keep a defendant from committing more crimes before trial is to set bail so high that he cannot obtain his release.

THE PROSECUTOR

The key administrative officer in the processing of cases is the prosecutor. Theoretically the examination of the evidence against a defendant by a judge at a preliminary hearing, and its reexamination by a grand jury, are important parts of the process. Practically they seldom are because a prosecutor seldom has any difficulty in making a prima facie case against a defendant. In fact most defendants waive their rights to preliminary hearings and much more often than not grand juries indict precisely as prosecutors ask them to. The prosecutor wields almost undisputed sway over the pretrial progress of most cases. He decides whether to press a case or drop it. He determines the specific charge against a defendant. When the charge is reduced, as it is in as many as two-thirds of all cases in some cities, the prosecutor is usually the official who reduces it.

In the informal, noncriminal, non-adversary juvenile justice system there are no "magistrates" or "prosecutors" or "charges," or, in most instances, defense counsel. An arrested youth is brought before an intake officer who is likely to be a social worker or, in smaller communities, before a judge. On the basis of an informal inquiry into the facts and circumstances that led to the arrest and of an interview with the youth himself, the intake officer or the judge decides whether or not a case should be the subject of formal court proceedings.

If he decides it should be, he draws up a petition, describing the case. In very few places is bail a part of the juvenile system; a youth whose case is referred to court is either sent home with orders to reappear on a certain date, or remanded to custody. This decision, too, is made by the screening official. Thus, though these officials work in a quite different environment and according to quite different procedures from magistrates and prosecutors, they in fact exercise the same kind of discretionary control over what happens before the facts of a case are adjudicated.

THE PLEA AND THE SENTENCE

When the prosecutor reduces a charge it is ordinarily because there has been "plea bargaining" between him and a defense attorney. The issue at stake is how much the prosecutor will reduce his original charge or how lenient a sentence he will recommend, in return for a plea of guilty. There is no way of judging how many bargains reflect the prosecutor's belief that a lesser charge or sentence is justified and how many result from the fact that there may be in the system at any one time ten times as many cases as there are prosecutors or judges or courtrooms to handle them, should every one come to trial.

In form, a plea bargain can be anything from a series of careful conferences to a hurried consultation in a courthouse corridor. In content it can be anything from a conscientious exploration of the facts and dispositional alternatives available and appropriate to a defendant, to a perfunctory deal. If the interests of a defendant are to be properly protected while his fate is being thus invisibly determined, he obviously needs just as good legal representation as the kind he needs at a public trial. Whether or not plea bargaining is a fair and effective method of disposing of criminal cases depends heavily on whether or not defendants are provided early with competent and conscientious counsel.

Plea bargaining is not only an invisible procedure but, in some jurisdictions, a theoretically unsanctioned one. In order to satisfy the court record, a defendant, his attorney, and the prosecutor will at the time of sentencing often ritually state to a judge that no bargain has been made. Plea bargaining may be a useful procedure, especially in congested urban jurisdictions, but neither the dignity of the law, nor the quality of justice, nor the protection of society from dangerous criminals is enhanced by its being conducted covertly.

In the juvenile system there is, of course, no plea bargaining in the sense described above. However, the entire juvenile process can involve extra-judicial negotiations about disposition. Furthermore, the entire juvenile process is by design invisible. Though intended to be helpful, the authority exercised often is coercive; juveniles, no less than adults, may need representation by counsel.

An enormously consequential kind of decision is the sentencing decision of a judge. The law recognizes the importance of fitting sentences to individual defendants by giving judges, in most instances, considerable latitude. For example the * * * New York Penal Code, which [went] into effect in autumn of 1967, empowers a judge to impose upon a man convicted of armed robbery any sentence between a 5-year term of probation and a 25-year term in prison.

Even when a judge has presided over a trial during which the facts of a case have been carefully set forth and has been given a probation report that carefully discusses a defendant's character, background, and problems, he cannot find it easy to choose a sentence. In perhaps nine-tenths of all cases there is no trial; the defendants are self-confessedly guilty.

In the lower or misdemeanor courts, the courts that process most criminal cases, probation reports are a rarity. Under such circumstances judges have little to go on and many sentences are bound to be based on conjecture or intuition. When a sentence is part of a plea bargain, which an overworked judge ratifies perfunctorily, it may not even be his conjecture or intuition on which the sentence is based, but a prosecutor's or a defense counsel's. But perhaps the greatest lack judges suffer from when they pass sentence is not time or information, but correctional alternatives. Some lower courts do not have any probation officers, and in almost every court the caseloads of probation officers are so heavy that a sentence of probation means, in fact, releasing an offender into the community with almost no supervision. Few States have a sufficient variety of correctional institutions or treatment programs to inspire judges with the confidence that sentences will lead to rehabilitation.

CORRECTIONS

The correctional apparatus to which guilty defendants are delivered is in every respect the most isolated part of the criminal justice system. Much of it is physically isolated; its institutions usually have thick walls and locked doors, and often they are situated in rural areas, remote from the courts where the institutions' inmates were tried and from the communities where they lived. The correctional apparatus is isolated in the sense that its officials do not have everyday working relationships with officials from the system's other branches, like those that commonly exist between policemen and prosecutors, or prosecutors and judges. It is isolated in the sense that what it does with, to, or for the people under its supervision is seldom governed by any but the most broadly written statutes, and is almost never scrutinized by appellate courts. Finally, it is isolated from the public partly by its invisibility and physical remoteness; partly by the inherent lack of drama in most of its activities, but perhaps most importantly by the fact that the correctional apparatus is often used or misused by both the criminal justice system and the public as a rug under which disturbing problems and people can be swept.

The most striking fact about the correctional apparatus today is that, although the rehabilitation of criminals is presumably its major purpose, the custody of criminals is actually its major task. On any given day there are well over a million people being "corrected" in America, two-thirds of them on probation or parole and one-third of them in prisons or jails. However, prisons and jails are where four-fifths of correctional money is spent and where nine-tenths of correctional employees work.

Furthermore, less than one-fifth of the people who work in State prisons and local jails have jobs that are not essentially either custodial or administrative in character. Many jails have nothing but custodial and administrative personnel. Of course many jails are crowded with defendants who have not been able to furnish bail and who are not considered by the law to be appropriate objects of rehabilitation because it has not yet been determined that they are criminals who need it.

What this emphasis on custody means in practice is that the enormous potential of the correctional apparatus for making creative decisions about its treatment of convicts is largely unfulfilled. This is true not only of offenders in custody but of offenders on probation and parole. Most authorities agree that while probationers and parolees need varying degrees and kinds of supervision, an average of no more than 35 cases per officer is necessary for effective attention; 97 percent of all officers handling adults have larger caseloads than that. In the juvenile correctional system the situation is somewhat better. Juvenile institutions, which typically are training schools, have a higher proportion of treatment personnel and juvenile probation and parole officers generally have lighter caseloads. However, these comparatively rich resources are very far from being sufficiently rich.

Except for sentencing, no decision in the criminal process has more impact on the convicted offender than the parole decision, which determines how much of his maximum sentence a prisoner must serve. This again is an invisible administrative decision that is seldom open to attack or subject to review. It is made by parole board members who are often political appointees. Many are skilled and conscientious, but they generally are able to spend no more than a few minutes on a case. Parole decisions that are made in haste and on the basis of insufficient information, in the absence of the parole machinery that can provide good supervision, are necessarily imperfect decisions. And since there is virtually no appeal from them, they can be made arbitrarily or discriminatorily. Just as carefully formulated and clearly stated law enforcement policies would help policemen, charge policies would help prosecutors and sentencing policies would help judges, so parole policies would help parole boards perform their delicate and important duties.

In sum, America's system of criminal justice is overcrowded and overworked, undermanned, underfinanced, and very often misunderstood. It needs more information and more knowledge. it needs more technical resources. It needs more coordination among its many parts. It needs more public support. It needs the help of community programs and institutions in dealing with offenders and potential offenders. It needs, above all, the willingness to reexamine old ways of doing things, to reform itself, to experiment, to run risks, to date. It needs vision.

Chapter Thirteen
Victims Compensation

Crime Victim Compensation - Frequently Asked Questions
At the time this was written, these were the qualifying numbers and qualifications:

What Benefits Are Available?

- Maximum award up to $15,000
- Funeral expenses are limited to $5,000
- Lost wages are limited to $500 per month
- Emergency awards up to $1,000

What Types of Expenses Can Be Compensated?

- Medical, dental and hospital services
- Mental health counseling and care
- Funeral/burial expenses
- Loss of earnings
- Loss of support to dependents
- Homemaker replacement services loss
- Eyeglasses, hearing aids and other prosthetic or medically necessary devices
- Certain other out-of-pocket expenses incurred as a result of the crime

Who Can File A Claim?

- A victim of a crime who has suffered physical injury as a result of:
    - a criminal attack
    - trying to stop a person committing a crime
    - trying to help a law enforcement officer
    - trying to help a victim of a crime
- Families and dependents of deceased victims
- Persons who are authorized to act on behalf of victims

What Are The Eligibility Requirements?

- The crime must have occurred in Wyoming on or after May 23, 1985
- The crime must be reported to law enforcement as soon as possible
- The victim or claimant must fully cooperate in the investigation and prosecution of the crime
- The claim must be filed within one (1) year of the injury or death.
- Federal crime victims are eligible to apply for compensation whether or not the crime falls under tribal, state, or federal jurisdiction
- No portion of the compensation shall benefit the offender in any way
- A victim whose own misconduct either caused or contributed to the criminal attack could be reduced or denied compensation

Who Is NOT Eligible?

- The offender and/or accomplice
- A victim convicted of a felony after applying for compensation
- An individual who is a victim of a criminal attack while confined in a prison or other correctional facility at the time of the crime
- A victim whose expenses are paid entirely by other sources
- Victims of monetary or property loss
- Victims seeking compensation only for pain and suffering

What If There Is Insurance Or Another Source to Cover Part of the Losses?

Insurance benefits must be used first. If insurance does not pay the entire amount, then you would be eligible to be compensated for what insurance does not cover. Compensation is a secondary source which pays for losses that are not paid by other sources such as:

- Health insurance
- Sick or vacation leave paid by an employer
- Disability insurance
- Indian Health Service
- Worker's Compensation
- Social Security

Does There Have To Be An Arrest Or Conviction Before Compensation Will Be Paid

- No.

What If Restitution Is Recovered From The Offender?

- In the event that the court orders the offender to make restitution, that portion of the restitution covering expenses paid by the compensation program must be reimbursed back to the compensation fund. If you recover money through a civil suit against the offender, you will be required to pay the compensation program for expenses that program paid on your behalf.

How Is The Claim Processed?

- Upon receipt of the application, an investigation is conducted to verify all the information. Law enforcement, witnesses, service providers, employers, etc. are contacted to substantiate the compensation application. It usually requires a minimum of 90 days to process an application.
- The division staff reviews the claim and decides if it qualifies for compensation and determines the amount(s) and category(s) the victim may be eligible for. The claims

specialist submits the completed claim to the division director for a decision.

- The division will notify you of the amount of the award. If the claim is denied or payment reduced, the reason will be provided in writing.
- If the claim is reduced or denied, the victim has the right to request an appeal within 30 days upon receipt of the decision.
- Emergency compensation (to cover basic, survival needs) can be awarded within a short period of time. It usually takes 10 working days to process an emergency request. No appeals are granted on emergency claims.

How Do I Apply?

You must file an application. You may follow the links listed at the bottom of this page to view the application instructions and to fill out an application form. When you have completed the form, print it out and send it to the address listed below. You may also obtain an application by calling the Division of Victim Services at (307) 777-7200. You may call collect. Applications are also available in your community at the following locations:

- law enforcement agencies
- domestic violence/ sexual assault agencies
- prosecuting attorney's offices
- victim assistance agencies

Chapter Fourteen
Death Notifications

One of the hardest things to do is to tell someone that a loved one has died. It is also one of the most rewarding things first responders can ever do. This chapter will give you a toolbox to reach into that will help ensure a successful notification is made. Before we start our look at death notifications we should define what a, "successful", death notification looks like.

It is important to note that throughout this chapter the person you are notifying is referred to as your client. This is done for several reasons. The first is that even though these calls can be the most emotional calls you will ever go on it is imminently important to be professional. *You are going to be changing people's lives forever.* You owe it to the family and support people you are giving this horrible news too to be professional. We refer to the family members and support people in this chapter as clients to remind you of your relationship to those people. It can also be helpful to remember that as in any business your client is king. Without a client you have no business.

A successful death notification is one in which the correct family member or loved one is notified about the correct deceased person in a timely fashion and useful tools are given to help the family or loved ones cope with the grief. Notice there is nothing in the definition about fixing the family member or loved one. There is also nothing in the definition about decreasing the grief or lessening the blow. Death notifications can be very complicated, volatile calls. If you focus on what the successful notification looks like from the beginning you have a much better chance of reaching that goal at the end of the call. First we should be at the beginning.

PREPARATION

Before you begin there are a few things that MUST be squared away. Make sure before you do anything that you have **gained permission** to do the death notification. This permission must be granted from the local coroner's office, your responding agency and the agency you represent. There simply isn't any room for free lancing when doing a death notification. An easy way to gain permission is to remind the agencies that you are highly trained and can free up the other agencies to respond to their duties. In some of these cases one or all of the other agencies may wish to respond with you or may deny your assistance. This is ok. Remember that you will generally need to work with these agencies in the future. There is no sense in making a rift in a relationship when there is no need to.

Gather all available information concerning the individual(s) who have died. This includes the following:
- Full name including middle initial
- Date of birth
- Social security number
- Address

- A contact number for the person who knows something about the incident as well as who told you to do the notification

IF ANOTHER AGENCY IS NOTIFYING SOMEONE FOR YOU…

Call back if coordinating with another agency for that agency to do the notification. Talk directly with the individuals who will be doing the notification. Explain to them _exactly_ what you want them to say. Remember that this your reputation on the line! Give them a _direct number_ for them to call you back once contact has been made and stay at that number. Ask them to _remain at the scene_ until a support network has been set up. The support network can be set up of any number of the following: friends, family, clergy, neighbors. Get their names and address for a follow-up call and thank you letter. DON'T FORGET to send out the thank you letter and call them back!

IF YOU ARE NOTIFYING SOMEONE FOR ANOTHER AGENCY…

Talk directly with the individual who is requesting the notification. Get names and address for follow-up confirmation and information. _Get confirmation_! If you are unsure about any part of the notification make sure and confirm with the folks who know. Ask the person who is asking you to do the notification for a direct contact number and ask them to _remain at the direct number_ as a resource. Call back and update the people asking you to do the notification until the notification is complete. Give your contact number for additional follow-up information. **_Partner with someone!_** Now is not the time to go solo. Remember that you are partnering with someone therefore inform them of the situation and include them in the process. Do the notification as a team. _Let an outside link know._ Safety is important. Keep in contact with your outside link at regular intervals and let them know where you're going and what your mission is.

ARRIVAL!!

Whenever possible NEVER use the phone to make a death notification. We live in an information age in which with extremely rare exceptions every jurisdiction has at least a law enforcement department that can do notifications for you if you can't do one in person. There are guidelines at the end of this chapter discussing the protocol for doing a notification over the phone.

Always be prepared to spend time. You are on you clients clock. Clear your schedule and be prepared to go the extra mile for your client. The key thing to remember is your mission which is to give the information to the right people about the right decedent and to begin the process of having your client start the walk toward self-sufficiency.

Identify your partner and yourself. This is an important part of the process. Most times the second you identify yourself your client will at the very least know that things are serious. If you don't identify yourself with the agency your with there can be doubt from you client as to the veracity of any of the information that is forthcoming. **_Don't fall apart!!_** It is perfectly reasonable at times to cry on a scene and show some emotion. If you overdo the emotion however you are putting yourself in a position of hindering any assistance you can give to your client. Remember, *it's all about your client who is the family members and support people you are notifying. It is not about you!!* Identify who you are speaking with and use the deceased person's name.

Gather information. Be specific. Confirm information. Ask, "Is this where first, middle, last name lives" if you are at the decedents house. Ask the person you are talking to initially what relationship they have to the deceased. **_Be positive_** that this is the right place and person before going on.

Prepare them. Ask if you may come into the house. Ask if anyone else is present and gather them all together. Have everyone *sit down.*

Be Clear!!! Keep your message clear and to the point. Use the words *died, dead, and injured.* Keep your voice *calm and steady.* Use the decedents name and listen to your client. The family may wish you to use a different name when referring to the decedent. Adjust to your clients wishes. Provide a resources number for your client.

Keep in mind Kubler Ross's 5 stages of grief. Kubler Ross developed the concept of the 5 stages of grief several decades ago as a way to help first responders performing death notification to remember reactions they can see on a scene. The 5 stages are *denial, anger, regret, depression, and acceptance.* It is important to remember that people float in and out of all of these stages and can go in and out of these stages for several years after the initial trauma.

Accept their response. We have seen every kind of reaction one can imagine. People react in highly differing ways. Remember that the information you just gave to your client is usually shocking but may not necessarily be. Keep in mind your safety and the safety of your client(s). If the reaction is obviously self destructive and potentially life threatening you and your partner must take action to change the situation. Now is not the time for long soliloquies Keep quiet and allow your client to digest the information you have given them. Be prepared to help them find information. Allow them to choose what comes next

THINGS NOT TO DO!!!

Don't lie to ease the pain. You must give them only information you have confirmed and have been allowed to give out.

Don't stop them from experiencing shock and grief. Crying is a natural thing in these cases. Screaming is a natural thing in these cases. Stopping your clients from reacting to grief tells them that they shouldn't be reacting that way and will prohibit the body's natural grief mechanisms to heal.

Don't keep talking. This is not a talk show.
Don't rationalize or minimalise. Clients need to feel free to relay their feelings and emotions. They won't communicate things if they feel like they can't.

Don't be argumentative. There is no constructive reason to get into a debate session with a client. Now is not the time for the O'Reilly Factor!

Don't talk about your experiences. Remember it is not about you. You may have experienced something equally horrific. You may have experienced something almost identical. Your experience is not their experience.

Don't talk about your personal beliefs. Remember it is about your client. If you go on about your belief system and faith structure you are taking valuable time away from your client that can be used by them to decompress. Remember also that your beliefs are not necessarily everyone else's beliefs. You do not want to engage your client in an argument.

THINGS YOU SHOULD BE DOING

Expect the unexpected. Grief is displayed in a wide variety of forms. You may see people in extreme shock. You may see people get extremely upset. You may have a need to have emergency medical services step in an evaluate your client. Be prepared for everything.

Remain Calm. It may seem as though your client is not watching your reactions. They are. You have to stay calm and focused to provide the best services to your client. If they see you falling apart they will take your lead.

Listen Carefully. Always be prepared to gather important information that can either aid in recovery for your client or aid in the investigation of the situation that is at hand.

Accept all responses. Be patient, supportive and do not judge.

Provide useful information. Gather as much information as you can prior to delivering the notification. Only give them information that answers their questions of the moment. Package the information you do give them in such a way that they can deal with it. Now is not the time to go into the gory details.

Be prepared. Do not answer questions you are not absolutely sure of. Defer to the proper authorities.

Be supportive of other agencies. Remember these folks are going to have to engage with the other agencies long after you are gone. You are setting the tone for future interactions.

Ask the parents before delivering information to children.

Give them stress reaction information. This will be given both verbally and in the form of a handout. If you don't have a handout, make one.

Remember ***These are normal reactions to an abnormal event.*** Encourage them to get support

Encourage physical health. The goal here is to get your clients back to their routines as quickly as possible.

Encourage positive memories and talking it out. Ask them to relay good memories of their loved one for you.

SETTING UP A SUPPORT SYSTEM

Family and friends. Do not force them to call people they will know who they are comfortable with. Tell them that is ok to tell Aunt Ethell to go away politely. Ask them if you can help call anyone. If you do call anyone to give them information always ask your client first if it is alright to give out their number to the person you are calling.

Think about clergy, doctors, and mental health counselors, any others that can help.

Only notify other if you are requested to do so!

SO WHEN DO I LEAVE???

Leave when sufficient support help arrives or if you are asked to leave by the client. If you are asked to stay by the client stay. If you are asked to escort your client to the scene, mortuary or hospital makes sure it is acceptable in your agency first. Prepare them for what they are going to see. NOTIFY THE DESTINATION SO THEY KNOW YOU ARE COMING.

Revisit on an individual basis. Do not get into the rescuer mentality. Remember the goal is to facilitate your client in working through the information you just gave them. YOU CAN'T FIX ANYONE!!!!

Chapter Fifteen
Self Care

STRESS MANAGEMENT: TEN SELF-CARE TECHNIQUES

*This brochure was shared at http://www.ucc.vt.edu/stdysk/stresmgt.html
by Virginia Polytechnic Institute and State University*

TO RELAX. Throughout the day, take "mini-breaks". Sit down and get comfortable. Slowly take in a deep breath; hold it; and then exhale very slowly. At the same time, let your shoulder muscles droop, smile, and say something positive like, "I am r-e-l-a-x-e-d." Be sure to get sufficient rest at night.

PRACTICE ACCEPTANCE. Many people get distressed over things they won't let themselves accept. Often, these are things that can't be changed, for example someone else's feelings or beliefs. If something unjust bothers you that is different. If you act in a responsible way, the chances are you will manage that stress effectively.

TALK RATIONALLY TO YOURSELF. Ask yourself what real impact the stressful situation will have on you in a day or in a week, and see if you can let the negative thoughts go. Think through whether the situation is <u>your</u> problem or the other person's. If it is yours, approach it calmly and firmly. If it is the other person's, there is not much you can do about it. Rather than condemning yourself with hindsight thinking like, "I should have...," think about what you can learn from the error and plan for the future. Watch out for perfectionism -- set realistic and attainable goals. Remember: everyone makes errors. Be careful of procrastination -- practice breaking tasks into smaller units to make it manageable, and practice prioritizing to get things done.

GET ORGANIZED. Develop a realistic schedule of daily activities that includes time for work, sleep, relationships, and recreation. Use a daily "thing to do " list. Improve your physical surroundings by cleaning your house and straightening up your office. Use your time and energy efficiently.

EXERCISE. Physical activity has always provided relief from stress. In the past, daily work was largely physical. Now that physical exertion is no longer a requirement for earning a living, we don't get rid of stress so easily. It accumulates very quickly. We need to develop a regular exercise program to reduce the effects of stress before it becomes distress. Try aerobics, walking, jogging, dancing, or swimming.

REDUCE TIME URGENCY. If you frequently check your watch or worry about what you do with your time, learn to take things a bit slower. Allow plenty of time to get things done. Plan your schedule ahead of time. Recognize that you can only do so much in a given period. Practice the notion of "pace, not race".

DISARM YOURSELF. Every situation in life does not require you to be competitive. Adjust your approach to an event according to its demands. You don't have to raise your voice in a simple discussion. Playing tennis with a friend does not have to be an Olympic trial. Leave behind you your "weapons" of shouting, having the last word, putting someone else down, and blaming.

QUIET TIME. Balance your family, social, and work demands with special private times. Hobbies are good antidotes for daily pressures. Unwind by taking a quiet stroll, soaking in a hot bath, watching a sunset, or listening to calming music.

WATCH YOUR HABITS. Eat sensibly -- a balanced diet will provide all the necessary energy you will need during the day. Avoid nonprescription drugs and avoid alcohol use -- you need to be mentally and physically alert to deal with stress. Be mindful of the effects of excessive caffeine and sugar on nervousness. Put out the cigarettes -- they restrict blood circulation and affect the stress response.

TALK TO FRIENDS. Friends can be good medicine. Daily doses of conversation, regular social engagements, and occasional sharing of deep feelings and thoughts can reduce stress quite nicely.

ABOUT STRESS--

Many people don't realize it, but stress is a very natural and important part of life. Without stress there would be no life at all! We need stress (eustress), but not too much stress for too long (distress). Eustress helps keep us alert, motivates us to face challenges, and drives us to solve problems. These low levels of stress are manageable and can be thought of as necessary and normal stimulation.

Distress, on the other hand, results when our bodies over-react to events. It leads to what has been called a "fight or flight" reaction. Such reactions may have been useful in times long ago when our ancestors were frequently faced with life or death matters. Nowadays, such occurrences are not usual. Yet, we react to many daily situations as if they were life or death matters. Our bodies don't really know the difference between a saber-tooth tiger attacking and an employer correcting our work. How we perceive and interpret the events of life dictates how our bodies react. If we think something is very scary or worrisome, our bodies react accordingly.

When we view something as manageable, though, our body doesn't go haywire; it remains alert but not alarmed. The activation of our sympathetic nervous system (a very important part of our general nervous system) mobilizes us for quick action. The more we sense danger (social or physical), the more our body reacts. Have you ever been unexpectedly called upon to give an "off-the-cuff" talk and found that your heart pounded so loudly and your mouth was so dry that you thought you just couldn't do it? That's over-reaction.

Problems can occur when the sympathetic nervous system is unnecessarily over activated frequently. If we react too strongly or let the small over-reactions (the daily hassles) pile up, we may run into physical as well as psychological problems. Gastrointestinal problems (examples: diarrhea or nausea), depression, severe headaches, or relapse can come about from acute distress.

Insomnia, heart disease, and distress habits (examples: drinking, overeating, smoking, and using drugs) can result from the accumulation of small distresses.

What we all need is to learn to approach matters in more realistic and reasonable ways. Strong reactions are better reserved for serious situations. Manageable reactions are better for the everyday issues that we typically have to face.

REACTOR OR OVER-REACTOR?

Below are situations that cause stress in some people and distress in others. Imagine yourself in each one right now. How are you reacting?

- Driving your car in rush hour
- Getting a last minute work assignment
- Misplacing something in the house
- Having something break while you're using it
- Dealing with incompetence at work
- Planning your budget
- Being blamed for something
- Waiting in a long line at the grocery store

Chapter Sixteen

Elder Abuse

Every year, tens of thousands of elderly Americans are abused in their own homes, in relatives' homes, and even in facilities responsible for their care. You may suspect that an elderly person you know is being harmed physically or emotionally by a neglectful or overwhelmed caregiver or being preyed upon financially. By learning the signs and symptoms of elder abuse and how to act on behalf of an elderly person who is being abused, you'll not only be helping someone else but strengthening your own defenses against elder abuse in the future.

What is elder abuse

Your elderly neighbor

There's an elderly neighbor you've chatted with at civic meetings and block parties for years. When you see her coming to get her mail as you walk up the street, you slow down and greet her at the mailbox. She says hello but seems wary, as if she doesn't quite recognize you. You ask her about a nasty bruise on her forearm. Oh, just an accident, she explains; the car door closed on it. She says goodbye quickly and returns to the house. Something isn't quite right about her. You think about the bruise, her skittish behavior. Well, she's getting pretty old, you think; maybe her mind is getting fuzzy. But there's something else — something isn't right.

As elders become more physically frail, they're less able to stand up to bullying and or fight back if attacked. They may not see or hear as well or think as clearly as they used to, leaving openings for unscrupulous people to take advantage of them. Mental or physical ailments may make them more trying companions for the people who live with them.

Tens of thousands of seniors across the United States are being abused: harmed in some substantial way often people who are directly responsible for their care
More than half a million reports of abuse against elderly Americans reach authorities every year, and millions more cases go unreported.

Where does elder abuse take place?

Elder abuse tends to take place where the senior lives: most often in the home where abusers are apt to be adult children; other family members such as grandchildren; or spouses/partners of elders. Institutional settings especially long-term care facilities can also be sources of elder abuse.

The different types of elder abuse

Abuse of elder's takes many different forms, some involving intimidation or threats against the elderly, some involving neglect, and others involving financial chicanery. The most common are defined below.

Physical abuse

Physical elder abuse is non-accidental use of force against an elderly person that results in physical pain, injury, or impairment. Such abuse includes not only physical assaults such as hitting or shoving but the inappropriate use of drugs, restraints, or confinement.

Emotional abuse

In emotional or psychological senior abuse, people speak to or treat elderly persons in ways that cause emotional pain or distress.

Verbal forms of emotional elder abuse include

- intimidation through yelling or threats
- humiliation and ridicule
- habitual blaming or scapegoating

Nonverbal psychological elder abuse can take the form of

- ignoring the elderly person
- isolating an elder from friends or activities
- terrorizing or menacing the elderly person

Sexual abuse

Sexual elder abuse is contact with an elderly person without the elder's consent. Such contact can involve physical sex acts, but activities such as showing an elderly person pornographic material, forcing the person to watch sex acts, or forcing the elder to undress are also considered sexual elder abuse.

Neglect or abandonment by caregivers

Elder neglect, failure to fulfill a caretaking obligation, constitutes more than half of all reported cases of elder abuse. It can be active (intentional) or passive (unintentional, based on factors such as ignorance or denial that an elderly charge needs as much care as he or she does).

Financial exploitation

This involves unauthorized use of an elderly person's funds or property, either by a caregiver or an outside scam artist.

An unscrupulous caregiver might

- misuse an elder's personal checks, credit cards, or accounts
- steal cash, income checks, or household goods
- forge the elder's signature

- engage in identity theft

Typical rackets that target elders include

- Announcements of a "prize" that the elderly person has won but must pay money to claim
- Phony charities
- Investment fraud

Healthcare fraud and abuse

Carried out by unethical doctors, nurses, hospital personnel, and other professional care providers, examples of healthcare fraud and abuse regarding elders include

- Not providing healthcare, but charging for it
- Overcharging or double-billing for medical care or services
- Getting kickbacks for referrals to other providers or for prescribing certain drugs
- Overmedicating or under medicating
- Recommending fraudulent remedies for illnesses or other medical conditions
- Medicaid fraud

Signs and symptoms of elder abuse

At first, you might not recognize or take seriously signs of elder abuse. They may appear to be symptoms of dementia or signs of the elderly person's frailty — or caregivers may explain them to you that way. In fact, many of the signs and symptoms of elder abuse do overlap with symptoms of mental deterioration, but that doesn't mean you should dismiss them on the caregiver's say-so.

General signs of abuse

The following are warning signs of some kind of elder abuse:

- Frequent arguments or tension between the caregiver and the elderly person
- Changes in personality or behavior in the elder

If you suspect elderly abuse, but aren't sure, look for clusters of the following physical and behavioral signs.

Signs and symptoms of specific types of abuse

Physical abuse
- Unexplained signs of injury such as bruises, welts, or scars, especially if they appear symmetrically on two side of the body
- Broken bones, sprains, or dislocations
- Report of drug overdose or apparent failure to take medication regularly (a prescription has more remaining than it should)
- Broken eyeglasses or frames

- Signs of being restrained, such as rope marks on wrists
- Caregiver's refusal to allow you to see the elder alone

In addition to the general signs above, indications of emotional elder abuse include

Emotional abuse
- Threatening, belittling, or controlling caregiver behavior that you witness
- Behavior from the elder that mimics dementia, such as rocking, sucking, or mumbling to oneself

Sexual abuse
- Bruises around breasts or genitals
- Unexplained venereal disease or genital infections
- Unexplained vaginal or anal bleeding
- Torn, stained, or bloody underclothing

Neglect by caregivers or self-neglect
- Unusual weight loss, malnutrition, dehydration
- Untreated physical problems, such as bed sores
- Unsanitary living conditions: dirt, bugs, soiled bedding and clothes
- Being left dirty or un-bathed
- Unsuitable clothing or covering for the weather
- Unsafe living conditions (no heat or running water; faulty electrical wiring, other fire hazards)
- Desertion of the elder at a public place

Financial exploitation
- Significant withdrawals from the elder's accounts
- Sudden changes in the elder's financial condition
- Items or cash missing from the senior's household
- Suspicious changes in wills, power of attorney, titles, and policies
- Addition of names to the senior's signature card
- Unpaid bills or lack of medical care, although the elder has enough money to pay for them
- Financial activity the senior couldn't have done, such as an ATM withdrawal when the account holder is bedridden
- Unnecessary services, goods, or subscriptions

Healthcare fraud and abuse
- Duplicate billings for the same medical service or device
- Evidence of overmedication or under medication
- Evidence of inadequate care when bills are paid in full
- Problems with the care facility:
  - Poorly trained, poorly paid, or insufficient staff
  - Crowding
  - Inadequate responses to questions about care

Risk factors for elder abuse

It's difficult to take care of a senior when he or she has many different needs, and it's difficult to be elderly when age brings with it infirmities and dependence. Both the demands of care giving and the needs of the elder can create situations in which abuse is more likely to occur.

Risk factors among caregivers

Many nonprofessional caregivers — spouses, adult children, other relatives and friends — find taking care of an elder to be satisfying and enriching. But the responsibilities and demands of elder caregiving, which escalate as the elder's condition deteriorates, can also be extremely stressful. The stress of elder care can lead to mental and physical health problems that make caregivers burned out, impatient, and unable to keep from lashing out against elders in their care.

Among caregivers, significant risk factors for elder abuse are

- inability to cope with stress (lack of resilience)
- depression, which is common among caregivers
- lack of support from other potential caregivers
- the caregiver's perception that taking care of the elder is burdensome and without psychological reward
- substance abuse

Even caregivers in institutional settings can experience stress at levels that lead to elder abuse. Nursing home staff may be prone to elder abuse if they lack training, have too many responsibilities, are unsuited to care giving, or work under poor conditions.

The elder's condition and history

Several factors concerning elders themselves, while they don't excuse abuse, influence whether they are at greater risk for abuse:

- The intensity of an elderly person's illness or dementia
- Social isolation; i.e., the elder and caregiver are alone together almost all the time
- The elder's role, at an earlier time, as an abusive parent or spouse
- A history of domestic violence in the home
- The elder's own tendency toward verbal or physical aggression

In many cases, elder abuse, though real, is unintentional. Caregivers pushed beyond their capabilities or psychological resources may not mean to yell at, strike, or ignore the needs of the elders in their care.

Reporting elder abuse

If you are an elder who is being abused, neglected, or exploited, tell at least one person. Tell your doctor, a friend, or a family member whom you trust. Other people care and can help you.

You can also call **Eldercare Locator** at **1-800-677-1116**.

The person who answers the phone will refer you to a local agency that can help. The Eldercare Locator answers the phone Monday through Friday, 9 am to 8 pm, Eastern Time.

How do I report suspected elder abuse?

The 500,000 to 1,000,000 reports of elder abuse recorded by authorities every year (the vast majority of which are proven to be true) are only the tip of the iceberg; according to data from different states, for every case of elder abuse reported, another 12 or 13 are not. Accordingly there's a great need for people to report suspected abuse.

In every state, physical, sexual, and financial abuses targeting elders that violate laws against assault, rape, theft, and other offenses are punishable as crimes. With some variation among states, certain types of emotional elder abuse and elder neglect are subject to criminal prosecution, depending on the perpetrators' conduct and intent and the consequences for the victim.

States differ on who is *required* to report suspected elder abuse (there's no federal standard), though the categories of mandatory reporters are expanding. Typically, medical personnel, nursing home workers, peace officers, emergency personnel, public officials, social workers, counselors, and clergy are listed as mandatory reporters, and that responsibility is spreading to financial institutions and other entities that work with seniors.

While it's important for elders to seek refuge from abuse, either by calling a local agency or telling a doctor or trusted friend, many seniors don't report the abuse they face even if they're able. Many fear retaliation from the abuser, while others believe that if they turn in their abusers, no one else will take care of them. When the caregivers are their children, they may be ashamed that their children are behaving abusively or blame themselves: "If I'd been a better parent when they were younger, this wouldn't be happening." Or they just may not want children they love to get into trouble with the law.

The first agency to respond to a report of elderly abuse, in most states, is **Adult Protective Services (APS)**. Its role is to investigate abuse cases, intervene, and offer services and advice. Again, the power and scope of APS varies from state to state. However, every state has at least one toll-free elder abuse hotline or helpline for reporting elder abuse in the home, in the community, or in nursing homes and other long-term care facilities. In addition, information and referral are also available from the national **Eldercare Locator: 1-800-677-1116**

Preventing elder abuse and neglect

We can help reduce the incidence of elder abuse, but it'll take more effort than we're making now. Preventing elder abuse means doing three things:

- Listening to seniors and their caregivers
- Intervening when you suspect elder abuse
- Educating others about how to recognize and report elder abuse

What you can do as a caregiver to prevent elder abuse

If you're overwhelmed by the demands of caring for an elder, do the following:

- Request help, from friends, relatives, or local respite care agencies, so you can take a break, if only for a couple of hours.
- Find an adult day care program.
- Stay healthy and get medical care for yourself when necessary.
- Adopt stress reduction practices.
- Seek counseling for depression, which can lead to elder abuse.
- Find a support group for caregivers of the elderly.
- If you're having problems with drug or alcohol abuse, get help.

And remember, elder abuse help lines offer help for caregivers as well. Call a helpline if you think there's a possibility you might cross the line into elder abuse.

What you can do as a concerned friend or family member

- Watch for warning signs that might indicate elder abuse. If you suspect abuse, *report it*.
- Take a look at the elder's medications. Does the amount in the vial jive with the date of the prescription?
- Watch for possible financial abuse. Ask the elder if you may scan bank accounts and credit card statements for unauthorized transactions.
- Call and visit as often as you can. Help the elder consider you a trusted confidante.
- Offer to stay with the elder so the caregiver can have a break — on a regular basis, if you can.

How you can protect yourself, as an elder, against elder abuse

- Make sure your financial and legal affairs are in order. If they aren't, enlist professional help to get them in order, with the assistance of a trusted friend or relative if necessary.
- Keep in touch with family and friends and avoid becoming isolated, which increases your vulnerability to elder abuse.
- If you are unhappy with the care you're receiving, whether it's in your own home or in a care facility, *speak up*. Tell someone you trust and ask that person to report the abuse, neglect, or substandard care to your state's elder abuse helpline or long term care ombudsman, or make the call yourself.

Finally, if you aren't in a position to help an elder personally, you can volunteer or donate money to the cause of educating people about elder abuse, and you can lobby to strengthen state laws and policing so that elder abuse can be investigated and prosecuted more readily. The life you save down the line may be your own.

Appendix

Stalking Resource Center

American Medical Association

John Hopkins

Mid Valley Women's Crisis Service

US Department of Justice

Gavin DeBecker and Associates

Theoretical Perspectives of Victimology

Critical Incident Stress Foundation

American Psychiatric Association

National Mental Health Association

American Psychological Association

World Health organization

National Crime Victimization Survey

Virginia polytechnic Institute

Eldercare Locator

CPSIA information can be obtained
at www.ICGtesting.com
Printed in the USA
LVHW021615110719
623803LV00015BA/452/P